A Tobacco Farmer's Daughter

By

Linda Hamlett Childress

© 2002 by Linda Hamlett Childress. All rights reserved.

No part of this book may be reproduced, stored in a retrieval system, or transmitted by any means, electronic, mechanical, photocopying, recording, or otherwise, without written permission from the author.

ISBN: 1-4033-1906-5 (Electronic)
ISBN: 1-4033-1907-3 (Softcover)
ISBN: 1-4033-1908-1 (Dustjacket)

This book is printed on acid free paper.

1stBooks - rev. 07/18/02

This collection of stories I dedicate to my *mama*, who never let me give up on this dream of mine. I also dedicate this to my daughter, *Ashley* who inspires me with her positive attitudes and common sense.

My mama

My Daddy

Acknowledgements

I would first like to thank my mama and daddy, Harry Lee and Jane Hamlett, for without them I would have *no* stories to tell. I would like to especially thank my mama for her continued support and encouragement during this project. Thanks also to my sisters Cathy, Janet and Kelly who shared many of these memories with me. Thanks to Jamie and Cody for their creative input.

Thanks to my bosses, Drs Coots, Ward, and Haley for their interest in my stories. Thanks C3! I also offer a big thanks to my co-workers Angie, Danielle, Tonia and my fellow hygienists for their true interest in this project. Thanks Angie for her unassuming friendship and support. To my patients I give my heart-felt thanks, as you are the ones who hear *all* my stories and *must* suffer through them because I have my hands in your mouths!

Thanks to Ron Sachs for being kind enough to proof read and give me his honest opinion of my little book.

Thanks to Johnnie Johns, my lake buddy, for spending hours telling me his own life stories and inspiring me to tell my own. (I'll miss you my friend)

Thanks to Steve, my husband of almost twenty years for tolerating all my "projects"!

Ashley, *you* are my daily inspiration.

Contents

- The Joy of Modern Technology 1
- Farm Flowers 15
- Tractor Driving Lessons 18
- Spring 22
- Mornings in the Plant Bed 26
- The Fields in spring 29
- Time for Planting 32
- School Days and Summer Vacations 37
- The Hilling Hoe 40
- Sucker Plucker 43
- Mishaps 45
- Whoopings 50
- Winter Fun 55
- Craptown Store 60
- Farm Animals 63
- Moving *Pipes* 67
- Blessed Rain and Scary Storms 71
- Mama 73
- The Garden 79

- Lessons from Daddy 81
- Daddy's Antics 84
- Silence 86
- Soul Searching 88
- Pulling Tobacco 92
- The Packing House 98
- Summers End 102

"The third barn"

Brief History

Before I begin entertaining you with my tobacco farm stories, I would like to paint you a picture, a picture of how I envisioned the tobacco farm that I was raised on. I'd like to begin by telling you a little about my mama and daddy.

My daddy, named Harry Lee Hamlett was born on April 29th, 1937 the ninth of ten children. He was born in the family home, affectionately referred to as the "big house" in Charlotte County. His parents were Harry James Hamlett and Ollie Jane Blackstock. Grandpa Hamlett ran the farm and a sawmill while grandma kept the home fires burning, literally!

My mama, Nellie Jane Martin was born on July 20th, 1940 in Appomattox County, the only daughter of Harry Clinton Martin and Bessie Hopson Roark. Grandpa Martin was a gifted carpenter by trade while Grandma Martin took care of the five children and as Grandma Hamlett did, kept the home fires burning.

In Elizabeth City North Carolina, with my daddy's sister Betty and her husband Troy looking on, my mama and daddy were married, June 4th, 1960. Mama was a mere babe at nineteen years of age and daddy was twenty-two.

They started their married life in a tiny blue and white trailer put next to the "big house" on the Hamlett family farm. They had no electricity and certainly no indoor plumbing. The "big house" was built a good distance from the main road, nestled in the woods. Beside the "big house" were a smoke house, a corn shed and a "johney house" out in the nearby pasture.

Eight months later they made the big move into a whitewashed three-room house *close* to the main road, but still on the farm. Their little house was surrounded by acres and acres of rich, open farmland, ponds and framed with dense wooded areas.

I recently found out the house they moved into had been occupied by many members of the Hamlett family.

Their home was down-to-earth, having only one bedroom, a living room and a kitchen with a back porch attached. *Simple* it was, but it was home.

I continue now with a brief chronological history of the farm:

My daddy recalls that bitter winter day in 1966 when he purchased the farm from his mama. He tenderly recalls her standing there in her old, long gray coat with her little black purse hanging from the crook of her arm. She was then in her 60's and not as strong as she once was. Grandma had a number of strokes and passed away twelve years later in her daughter's home in Arlington, Virginia. She was many miles from the farm home she so loved and longed to get back to.

1934 or 1935- my granddaddy, H.J. Hamlett purchased the farm for $1300.00 at a public auction. It was previously owned by Tom Canada.

1950- My daddy's brother Hugh purchased the farm for $5000.00.

1952- The farm was bought back from Uncle Hugh by my granddaddy for $5000.00.

1966- My daddy purchased the farm from his mother four years after his daddy passed away.

After purchasing the farm at auction, my granddaddy raised a small amount of corn, wheat, peanuts and chickens. He also ran a small sawmill. My granddaddy might have been described as the proverbial jack-of-all-trades and the master of none. He passed on to greener pastures in 1962 after a long battle with leukemia, just one month before I was born.

After daddy acquired the two hundred acre farm, He didn't really know what to do with it. (By then he was running a sawmill with his older brother Arnie). With my daddy's help, *mama* started her first crop of tobacco. One whole acre! Her crop quickly grew to fifteen acres; by 1997 her crop had grown to seventy-five acres.

I have countless stories about my childhood on the farm from the 60's to my treasured visits now in the new millennium. I hope you will take a step back in time and unite with me. These stories are for those of you who share some of these same memories and also for those of you who were not so privileged as to have had the farm experience. By sharing these stories and pictures I hope to bring you just a little closer to the farm life and to this "tobacco farmer's daughter.

Mama and Daddy 1959

Harry Lee, Jane, Betty and Troy
Wedding Day 1960

Larry and Jane with their parents Harry and Bessie Martin

Harry James and Ollie Jane Hamlett

Forward

The awesome beauty of our tobacco farm has always overwhelmed me, two hundred acres of dense woods, rolling green pastures, sandy fields and crisp clean air.

Growing up, I often set out to find a quiet place to rest on a hillside. I'd look upward at the blue sky and gaze at the puffy clouds moving in that gentle country breeze. I still feel the warmness of the sun on my upturned face. As serene as all that sounds, I still wondered if I'd *ever* escape the imprisonment of that tobacco farm and make my way out into the *real* world where I didn't get filthy everyday and could sleep late on Saturdays! *We* didn't have a summer vacation at the beach or days at the pool, and we *certainly* didn't sleep in on Saturday morning. Nope, not if you were a tobacco farmers daughter!

Looking back, I am *so* grateful for all the life lessons I learned on the farm. When you are a kid and later a teenager, tobacco farming is not what you had in mind for an *electrifying* summer vacation.

Let's now commence that stroll down memory lane and let me share some farm stories, especially of the tobacco farm. I hope this will paint a picture for you; a picture that shows that tobacco is not *all* about controversy and health hazards, but a life, a livelihood and a bouquet of colorful memories for *this country girl.*

I certainly found the old cliché, "you can take the girl out of the country, but you can't take the country out of the girl", to be so utterly true!

Tobacco Fields
1966

1) The Joy of Modern Technology

As we all know, being a child is a *wonderful* thing. One wonderful thing is "not knowing" if you are poor or if your parents are just behind the times. I'd say we were a little *unhurried* in catching up with modern technology.

Memories for me begin was I was age six or so. My three sisters and I shared an undersized room that housed a lone double bed. I sometimes found myself sleeping at the foot of that bed or on our old lumpy couch. Our garden bathroom was a lonesome "johney house" hidden in the back yard. It wasn't a fancy "johney", just a two-holer! It catered to more than just *us*, it housed spiders, bees and snakes and oh, that smell! I don't recall being brave enough to use the "johney" very often. That big black hole was quite frightening for a kid with a little butt!!

You might be wondering *what* I used if not the "johney"? Well, I had a favorite bush at the edge of the yard, far enough away as not to offend anyone, but close enough to the house to feel safe! In the daylight I went into the woods to do my business. "You gotta do what cha gotta do!"

When I *did* brave out there I always faced the issue of toilet paper. Heck, for awhile I didn't even know there was such a thing as a roll of squeezable soft paper designed the wipe the…

What I *did* find in the "johney house" was the old Sears and Roebuck catalog. Yes, it's *really* true. It wasn't in there to browse through, if you get my drift. I did feel quite proud of myself when I discovered that by folding and crunching a page over and over the paper became quite soft and therefore bearable. Of course after using leaves from a tree or whatever was available in the woods, the pages of the Sears and Roebuck catalog were quite a luxury.

Late at night I didn't *dare* venture to the johney house or to the dark and scary woods to do my business. At night mama put the white enamel "pot", also known as a chamber pot, on the back porch for the whole family to use, daddy included. Many times, *much to my dismay*, that "pot" would turn over when I tried to sit on it! What a mess! When the pot *didn't* get turned over poor mama got the pleasure of emptying it in the mornings. After being used by six people you can imagine the rancid smell! So, I am appreciative of modern technology!

Hot water *in* the house was another luxury we did not partake of in my early days. A double stainless steel sink in the kitchen only ran cold water. The pipes *often* froze in the winter due to lack of insulation. There is nothing like getting ready for school and finding that not only do you not have hot water, you don't have *any* water!! "Mama, can I stay home"?? Well, no…anyway daddy would cuss and mama would follow him outside with a light bulb on an extension cord to help thaw the pipes so that precious water ran freely once more.

Mama recalls one year in particular when the old, rusty pipe in the pump house "froze up". The pump house looks like a little out building with a tin roof. To gain access to the pipes you had to slide that tin roof off and climb up and over.

Daddy wasn't around that particular day to help, so my Grandma gave mama some ideas about defrosting the pipe. Grandma told mama to take hot ashes from the wood stove and put them in a bucket. She then told her to hold the bucket of hot ashes under the frozen pipe. Not such a great idea after all, those hot ashes touched the frozen pipe and that pipe "sprung a large leak!" Mama quickly covered the hole with her thumb and sat there inside the cold pump house wondering what the *heck* she was going to do! Daddy was working at the sawmill and grandma was two miles away; all the way down at the "big house"! Mama just squatted there with her thumb over the pipe pondering what she should do. Fortunately she heard a truck "pulling in." Mama then started hollerin' to get the attention of whoever it was. The truck was delivering farm material from Southern States. The driver followed the sound of the hollerin' and found mama crouched inside the pump house with her finger over the busted pipe. (What a sight that must have been.) He happened to have some electrical tape in his truck. Mama was ecstatic to see somebody. She took her finger off the busted pipe and got out of the pump house as quickly as she could. The Southern States man then jumped in and taped that hole right up! The Southern States man saves the day!

Are you wondering how, without an indoor bathroom, or the luxury of hot running water, we bathed? With a little galvanized tub, that's how. I can still hear the clank of the handles as mama dragged it from atop the pump house. She would heat up the water in a big pot on the gas stove and fill the tub. We girls then took our baths, one at a time. Yes, in the same water. Ivory soap made that bearable, not because it was a superior soap or that it floated, but because it made the water very white therefore you couldn't see the dirty water!

That galvanized tub was more than just a bathtub for us; it was also a source of summer entertainment. Since we had no pool to go to we made our own! With my sisters help we would heave the tub off the top of the pump house and hook up the garden hose. *Very* cold well water flowed into the tub and we had ourselves a pool! We fought over who would "swim" first!

On washday that old galvanized tub held the rinse water. It was put in a kitchen chair behind the wringer washer. Clothes were hand fed through the wringer into the tub of clean rinse water. The clothes were then fed back through the ringer to squeeze out the excess water. Laundry was an exhausting all day job. Mama had five clotheslines and they were *all* full on washday! I'll admit there is nothing like the smell of clothes dried on the clothesline in that fresh country air.

That good ole tub was also used when the garden "came in". We hauled tons potatoes and other vegetables in it. When the tub was *full* of potatoes it took two of us to haul it to the house. We, of course, were whining all the way with the weight of it.

My final memory of that galvanized tub was a not so cheerful one. It was late one summer night in the late 60's. I awoke to find the lights ablaze in the house and a neighbor sitting with us. I wondered, "What the heck was going on", as I made my way past the kitchen to the back porch to take a look. At that moment I realized Cathy, my oldest sister was not around. Then I saw the tub. It was filled with bright red blood! The blood, I found out, was from an uncontrollable nosebleed. Cathy's blood was in that tub.

My mama and daddy had tried in vain to stop the bleeding, but finally felt it was beyond anything they could do. They met the Brookneal rescue squad along the way for a quick trip to the emergency room. Fortunately, the bleeding was stopped in the ambulance and Cathy didn't go to the hospital after all. All in all that was an exciting, scary night and another memory of that ole *galvanized tub*. How versatile it was.

Around 1975 we girls were fast becoming teenagers. We really wished for an indoor bathroom with a *real* tub, a mirror on the wall and an honest to goodness toilet! I also longed for some PRIVACY! A funny thing was all my friends thought it was neat to come to our house and take a bath in the kitchen! When I went to *their* houses I didn't know what to do in the bathroom! You know, I didn't know how to run a bath? I learned how to flush in elementary school. I did learn something in my first try at first grade!

My daddy didn't see any real *need* for an indoor bathroom. He thought we were getting along just fine without *that* piece of modern technology.

One day he looked at his four growing daughters and realized how challenging it had become for us to do simple things, like wash our hair or just go to the bathroom. We now needed some privacy. We were becoming teenagers and daddy spent a lot of time trying not to walk in on us while we were in the kitchen taking our sink or tub baths! By this time my sister, Cathy, and I were much too big for the tub. Around 1975 daddy, bit the bullet, and hired someone to add a bedroom and thank you Jesus, a bathroom, complete with *hot* water and a toilet that flushed. I recall seeing the construction underway from the school bus and how all the kids were asking me what we were building. I was *so* full of pride. One might have thought we were building a whole new house, not just two small rooms.

The first bath in our new *indoor* facility was so very exciting, except for daddy's constant fear of the well "running dry". In the beginning we had to shower together or run only about an inch of water in the tub. To this day I have difficulty filling a tub completely without a guilty conscience. I have now developed a fetish for bathrooms and must have at least *two* at my disposal at *all* times!

After the addition was added to our house, my sister Janet and I shared a room. Cathy and Kelly, the oldest sister and youngest sister, shared another. Things were starting to look up for this tobacco farmer's daughter!

Everyone in the family appreciated the new addition except daddy. He tried to steer clear of it and use the good old reliable "johney house". It only took a few dozen bees waiting above the outhouse door to get daddy to give indoor plumbing a try. It didn't take long to hook him, but *then* he found he had a bigger problem, four daughters and a wife left little time for him to use this modern facility. It wasn't long before the contactor was back adding an additional bath and bedroom.

We had arrived, almost, and "you know what"? The well has, in spite of everything, "not gone dry"!

Now we had a washer, a dryer and two bathrooms, but no central air conditioning or heat! We had two other sources of heat. One source was the wood stove in the kitchen, which meant hauling wood from the woodpile to the back porch. We would stack the concrete back steps with wood, and then bring it inside to the "wood box". I didn't like bringing the wood in, but I did like chopping with an ax occasionally. I guess it was an adrenaline rush for me, a way to show my daddy I could do anything the boys could do.

Without central heating the cold mornings were tough. Mama would get up early and get the fire going in the wood stove and then wake us up. We would run to the kitchen and jockey for the warmest place in front of the stove. When the wood stove was not enough, mama would open the oven door to let us warm our hands and toes.

Heat in the living room came from an old brown oil circulator, which was our second source of heat. The blowing heat came from two vents at the bottom. I still recall watching mama warm her toes there after she had put us all to bed. I would watch her and suspect that this was a place where she did a lot of thinking. Heat also radiated from the *top* of the oil circulator. There we placed our wet hats and gloves to dry. Many times they didn't dry they scorched!

A favorite Christmas gift that I remember was my very own electric blanket, no more heating my toes by the stove and running for the bed! No more frosty sheets and shivering until I got warm. I'd turn my blanket on high before bed, let it get good and warm and crawl in. Um, oh how warm and snug it was. Leaving that warm place in the mornings was difficult.

The sweltering heat of summer brought a very different problem. We were always, hot, hot, and hot. We had a large green metal fan that took up the whole kitchen window. We girls would spend a lot of time in front of those swirling metal blades. We found our humming sounds within the fan amusing *and* we were getting cool at the same time. When mama wasn't looking we'd stick things into the blades of the fan. It sounded like a card in the spokes of a bicycle. It didn't take much to amuse us! At night each bedroom had one undersized window fan blowing cool air. Much quarrelling took place over who would sleep under that fan.

Years later we put a small window air-conditioning unit in the kitchen. Mama would close off the living room and back porch doors just so the kitchen was being cooled. Oh, it was heaven to come in from the sweltering heat of the field into that ice-cold kitchen!

The rest of the house was hot, but not the kitchen.

Mama could do her canning without sweating to death. After I moved away mama and daddy added central air and heat. My daddy still hangs on to that wood stove in the kitchen and I'll admit *he* has the last laugh when the power goes off. You can always depend on that wood stove for heat, no matter what!

The house I now live in seems to have a room for everything, sewing, cooking, and watching TV, exercising and so on. It seems the days are gone when we all gathered in a single room for activities. Gone also are the opportunities to make life long memories.

The kitchen was a place that was warm in the winter and cool in the summers, a place to share meals, to do homework, take baths and play games.

On Friday or Saturday nights my crazy aunts and uncles, or the neighbors, Roy and Joe Pollard, would come over to play "rook", a card game, with my folks. I remember the shouts of laughter, the innocent cursing, the snacks, drinks *and* the cigarette smoke. We talk about daddy cheating and of course *almost always* winning. While the adults played cards we kids were outside playing hide and seek in the dark or playing with the bats that circled around the security light. Yes, real bats. They are blind, but have a good sense of motion so; we would get empty cans from the house and hurl them into the air. The bats would swoop down after the can, sometimes a little too close for comfort. We ran screaming for cover when they swooped too low! Those were wonderful and innocent times. Sometimes when I am home, I look up at the bats that still circle around the security light, search around for an old can, and when no one is looking, toss that can in the air and watch the bats swoop down. A big smile spreads across my face and a warm feeling lifts my heart.

Our house has grown to three bedrooms, two baths, a back porch, a family room, a living room, a front porch and a deck. Having gone from a house sided with wood, to aluminum and now vinyl, from wood to furnace heat, we even got a color TV and a VCR!

I wonder if my daughter will have her own stories to tell, stories about the way things used to be. *My* memories are precious. I would not trade them for all the gold in California.

Linda Hamlett Childress

Playing in the "pool"

A Tobacco Farmer's Daughter

Linda Hamlett Childress

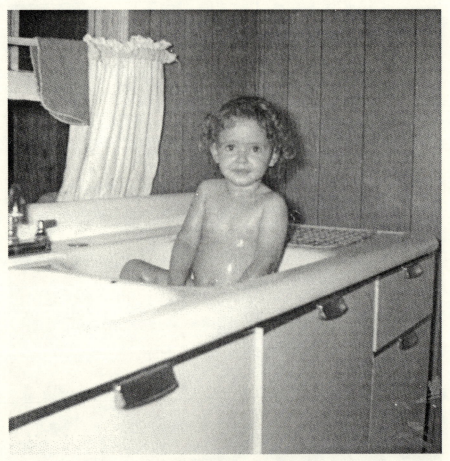

Bath time for Kelly
1969

My daughter, Ashley, in front of the old "johney house"
1992

Linda Hamlett Childress

I hope as you read these stories that you will, in at least one story, find yourself or see your own mama, daddy or your grandparents. If not, then just laugh or cry with me, follow me down memory lane.

Without further adieu let's get started.

2) Farm Flowers

At a very young age I started working in the tobacco fields.

Tobacco plants are usually bright green in color and sometimes grow six feet tall. A bunch of flowers sprout out at the top with smaller, "suckers" at the base of each leaf near the stalk. They sprout out after the plant has become mature and are damaging to the plant. This is not a "good" flower. In fact the "flowers and suckers" *have* to be removed (topped) or the weight of each leaf will be significantly reduced. So we painstakingly "topped" each plant and poured an oil appropriately named, "sucker plucker" (on top) to keep the flower from growing back. If you were too short to "top" then you had to "pull" the suckers at the bottom of the plant. City people thought the field looked neat with all those "flowers" on the plant, but to us tobacco farmers it only meant *more* work!

Another farm flower that caused me much misery was called the "morning glory". I soon came to loathe these beautiful flowered vines that swiftly snaked their way around the tobacco stalk, choking out life. Even though they were called morning "glories", I found nothing glorious about them. Plant after plant, row after row and acre after acre, we'd pull and do away with those vines. What a surprise when I found that people actually planted these vines on purpose and they paid good money for them! We would have been happy to give them all they wanted, for free! All they had to do was come pull them up!

Another flower around the farm that we avoided like the plague was what we called the "chigger weed". I usually found these "flowers" while playing near the edge of a field or next to the road somewhere.

I found if you played around these flowers too long you'd be scratching for a week. Ugly, red, itchy bumps would pop up after being around these "flowers". Again I was shocked when I attended a wedding and saw "chigger weeds" in the bride's bouquet. I felt I should knock them out of her hand and tell her to "run"! I was *quickly* educated and was told that those were not "chigger weeds"; they were called "Queen Ann's Lace", a wild "flower", not a weed! I was an adult before I learned that a *chigger* was just the *bug* that liked to hang out on this "wild flower". The *chigger bug* makes you itch, not the flower. Either way I associate them with itching! End of *that* story!

Poison Ivy was another farm flower that was hard to distinguish from other less volatile plants. I was an adult before I learned what to look for! These plants grew, it seemed everywhere; on the roadside heading to the house, in the woods, where I often did my business, and sometimes in mama's flowerbeds.

I spent *many* agonizing days *and* nights in my life scratching, crying and just plain miserable, thanks to these "flowers". I now stay away from *anything* that looks like this vine. Better safe than itchy! I can't help but add some old fashion remedies mama used to help with the itching of poison ivy. One was to make a paste out of baking soda and water. The paste was placed on the itchy spot, usually my feet. I found this remedy almost as useless as I did calamine lotion. One *crazy* remedy was one you *only* used as a last result, when you were *so close* to loosing your mind, and that involved Clorox! In my case, I was told to open the blisters, yes; you know what's coming. I took a towel and rubbed the blisters till I broke out in a cold sweat, then mama and later myself, would pour Clorox on the *open* sores. Oucheeeeeee. Ahhhhhhhh!!! The idea was to dry the sores out. I always felt better after this treatment *because* I was on the floor unconscious! (A natural reaction to all that pain.)

We had *some* pleasurable flowers on the farm. The wild daisy that grew in bunches almost everywhere you looked.

After a long hot day of work, I would walk miles away from the house and find a place to sit cross-legged in the tall grass, and pick those flowers. I would pluck their petals and sing, "he loves me, he loves me not". I kept picking flowers and pulling petals until the answer came out to my satisfaction, "He loves me".

Follow me now, with this last farm flower. I want you to *see* it, *smell* it and *taste* it.

Imagine a large patch of honeysuckle.

You have walked through the woods and into a clearing. There the flowers bloom in tangled masses near the pond.

The sky is blue; the sun is warm on your back as you find a place to sit. There is a slight breeze blowing in your face. Upon the breeze you smell that sweet scent of honeysuckle. Take a *deep* breath. Ahhh, can you smell it? Okay, good. Now settle down on the warm ground and pull a few of those honeysuckles off the stem. Break the base off one of the flowers and *slowly* pull the nectar from the flower. Now put the tiny drop on you tongue. Sweet isn't it? Don't *ever* miss a chance to stop and smell the flowers or even stop and *taste* the flowers!

3) Tractor Driving Lessons

Many jobs have to be learned when working on the tobacco farm, or *any* type farm for that matter. After graduating from weed pulling my daddy decided it was time I learned to drive the tractor. This was not a *choice* as much as it was a necessity.

Daddy selected the smallest tractor, a blue Massey Ferguson diesel to teach me on. I was about ten years old at the time. With my heart pounding loudly in my ears, I climbed aboard "old blue". I was shown neutral gears, the clutch, brake and the gas handle. Tractors don't have the gas peddle on the floor like cars and trucks; they have a handle behind the steering wheel. Daddy was not very patient and not likely to "tell" me how to drive this thing more than twice, so, with hands shaking I gripped the steering wheel and put my foot on the clutch. I turned the tiny key and the motor *roared* to life. Now what!!

Oh, how my knees were knocking.

Gingerly I shifted into first gear as instructed. "That went well", I thought. "Now gently ease your foot off the clutch." "*Gently*", daddy yelled, as I lurched forward and slammed on the brakes! Now I was *really* nervous and I wanted to cry so badly. On my second try, I once again put the tractor into first gear and *this* time really did *ease* off the clutch. With perfect grace that old diesel slowly, but surely, moved on down the road. It wasn't long before I got the nerve to take it out of *first* gear and run it full throttle. What power, I loved it. I was driving, and, I was only ten years old! *Life was good!*

A Tobacco Farmer's Daughter

Shortly thereafter I had to learn how to drive the other tractors.

The red Farmall had no key to start the motor, just a lever with a round finger-hook on the end, near the gearshift. The gears were shifted into neutral, while the right foot was lightly placed on the brake; the left foot on clutch then, with two hands, that lever was pulled. The engine usually came to life and I was off once more. We used the farmalls for plowing and the Fords for pulling the trailers or the tobacco planter.

I loved driving the tractor down the paved road at full throttle. The pavement was smooth and the tractor fast. My hair would fly in the wind. Many times people looked twice when they saw "girls" driving a tractor. We were after all "*girls*"!

We had fun with the tractor, but we also respected it for its power and its *danger*. What really got our attention was the death of a 16-year-old neighbor. He was riding on the fender of the tractor, and was wearing a long flannel shirt. The tail of his shirt became entangled in the wheel of the tractor. He was pulled off of the tractor and killed as the tire ran over him. I will never forget that day. I am since particularly careful when I ride shotgun on the tractor. I never wear long shirts or anything that might become entangled. What a shame I had to learn a lesson from that tragedy.

Farm related accidents happen daily. Unfortunately it seems to come with the territory.

When I go home today, I still take pleasure in taking the tractor for a spin. I always want to make sure I can still drive it! My daughter, Ashley, *the city girl*, found tractor-riding fun. My nephew, Cody and I, have, in the past, gone out and played "pretend plowing". That meant we took the tractor with the plow attached out to the field and plowed up weeds. It was all the same to us because we were plowing!

Rides around the farm on the tractor are still fun. Every now and then we hook a trailer up to one of the old tractors and take the kids for a ride. It's better than an amusement park ride and certainly more scenic. There are always plenty of smiles and laughs to go around!

A Tobacco Farmer's Daughter

Nine-month-old Cathy getting her first tractor driving lesson from daddy.
Summer 1961

4) Spring

When I lived on the farm, spring always brought a bag of mixed emotions. While it *did* mean warmer weather and an end too another school year, for the tobacco farmers' daughters, it meant non-stop work until October!

As the ground became warm we had to prepare the "beds" for the tobacco seeds. I can't say this was an awful job or too hard, I just wanted to be doing something else on this sunny Saturday morning in early April! I do vividly remember preparing those beds. My mom, sisters and I would walk over and over those beds throwing out rocks and any other trash that did not belong. As I walked back and forth I wondered if rocks had babies! One would think after years of use there would be no more rocks, but there always were. After throwing out the rocks we then raked the beds smooth. We then placed metal canisters of a chemical designed to kill bugs and weeds in designated areas. The beds were then covered with a heavy plastic. The ends of this heavy plastic were kept secure by using rocks, logs or anything we could find laying around that was weighty. An argument *always* broke out over the next step, which was releasing the chemical gas from the canisters into the soil. Mama, with four daughters, had become quite the diplomat and divided the job between the four of us. We took our shoes off so we didn't tear the plastic and walked out to our designated canisters. We placed one foot firmly on top of the canister and pushed until we heard the hissing sound of the gas being released. The plant beds then got to "rest" for a while. The gas would kill all the weeds and bugs. The soil would be almost sterile before we "seeded".

After a number of weeks it would be time to sow the tobacco seeds in the primed bed. The seeds came housed in a tiny metal tin and we kids were not allowed to even *look* at them, much less *touch* them! They cost daddy quite a lot of money and he guarded them closely. I rebelled once though. (Don't tell daddy) One day I saw the tin on top of the refrigerator and reached up to get it. My heart was pounding because I *knew* these were off limits. I opened the tin and peaked inside where I saw the *tiniest* seeds and *thousands* of them. I didn't look at them long, fearing I would get caught, but I was satisfied with my young self for breaking one of daddy's cardinal rules. Most of the time daddy kept the seeds stored safely in the glove compartment of his Ford pickup truck.

Before actually sowing the tiny black seeds, the tobacco beds required a little more work. The heavy plastic was removed and the empty chemical canisters were taken away. We once again raked and smoothed the beds and once again found more rocks! Mama then *ever so carefully* sowed those precious tiny black seeds. After sowing the seeds they had to be pressed into the loose dirt. To press the seeds into the loose soil we used a weighted press. It looked very much like the machine you see pressing freshly poured asphalt, except we didn't have the luxury of driving it; we had to push or pull it. It was very heavy and hard to get rolling. Until we were older that job was left to a stronger person. Back and forth that heavy wheel was pushed and pulled until the seeds were firmly packed. The plastic cover was then positioned back on the bed and small holes were punched in it so rain could seep through to the seeds. Every few days' mama and daddy would go "check the beds". They would loosen a corner and peep under the plastic to see if there was anything growing. I did find it neat when those tiny seeds turned into tiny plants and the soil took on a pretty moss green color.

When the plants were well on their way the plastic cover was removed and a cheesecloth type material put in its place. The plastic had acted like a greenhouse of sorts, holding in the heat and the moisture. The cheesecloth coverings were very delicate and I often tore them. (That got me in a little bit of trouble) Soon the little green sprouts became full-fledged plants and bulged under the cheesecloth. Rain was important to the well being of these plants. If Mother Nature did not supply us with enough rain then we had to irrigate. The gray metal irrigation pipes were hooked up to a pump that was located at the edge of the pond. Daddy had to say just the right combination of cuss words to get the pump running. Cussing and praying are two important tools to farming!

My sisters and I found playing under the irrigation sprinklers great fun and a break from work. We played a game called *dodge the water*. You wonder what that means I'll bet. Well, as the sprinkler spurted water we would run just ahead of it. The object was to not get caught by the sprays of stinky pond water. We *always* got wet and really didn't mind at all smelling like fishy pond water!

The tobacco plants continued to grow and become sturdy as other activities were going on around the farm. The fields had to be plowed and tilled. A tobacco farmer's work is *never* done.

A Tobacco Farmer's Daughter

Working mule
1966

5) Mornings in the Plant Bed

Lush, green tobacco plants now force the cheesecloth covering the beds to bulge. Planting time was now upon us. Very early in the morning in late spring we would begrudgingly get out of bed to go to the plant beds. We often found early spring mornings to be very nippy so we layered our clothes, old jeans, flannel shirt, t-shirt and a coat. Before hitting the back door we would grab a quick bowl of cereal and fight over the prize at the bottom of the box! We'd walk or ride one of the tractors down to the plant bed where we would often find our "help" already busy pulling the plants and gingerly placing them in a wooden crate. The cheesecloth cover had been pulled back exposing *hundreds* of green tobacco plants. I must admit the bed of green was a sight to see.

I spent a great deal time during my childhood trying to get *out* of work so I played *around* the plant beds as long as I could. Mama had a way of getting me on track. One line she used was, "the sooner we get started, the sooner we get finished". I use that bit of work ethic even today. Anyway, I would find me a spot and cozy down to begin pulling plants. Soon I was being yelled at, again. I was a quick study on selectively pulling plants. The bigger, stronger ones were to be *individually* pulled, *not* pulled in clumps! Pulling clumps seemed faster to me and the crates filled up faster! I was sharply reminded of the problems with clumps of plants. I'm *sure* I rolled my eyes and thought mom was being *overly* dramatic.

"How many plants do we have to pull", I often whined. I never figured out how my mama knew exactly how many crates to fill. She knew *exactly* how many crates to fill to keep us busy one full day. We were usually finished pulling plants out of the beds by eleven am. It was then time to take them to the fields to plant. Swinging by the house we picked up egg, cheese and tomato sandwiches smothered in mayonnaise. At that moment nothing else had ever tasted so good and *no one* could make that sandwich like my daddy.

One spring while pulling plants I found a sizeable patch of clovers. You don't think that is special do you? Well, these were *four-leaf* clovers! I had never seen so many in one spot. I frantically pulled them and this made my daddy *very* unhappy. He could have cared less about that patch of weeds! He had *no* idea what good fortune I had just happened upon! Even though I didn't pull them *all*, I felt I had enough for a *lifetime* of good fortune.

Year after year, we followed the same routine. The only thing that changed was our ages. Cathy and I found that dating didn't change the work hour's one bit!

Cathy recently reminded me of her senior prom. I was in the 10th grade and was also going to this prom. This particular Saturday had been planting tobacco and the day was growing shorter and shorter. Daddy would *not* let us leave early to get dressed. We were so mad but couldn't show our anger. Mama saw and felt our anguish, but was also powerless. We soon realized that the only way to finish early was to "*help*" the tobacco plant pile get smaller. From that moment on for every *one* we planted, *three* were thrown off to the side to the ground. We giggled to each other as we watched the trays become empty quickly. Daddy would have been *furious* had he known! Sorry Daddy!

Sweaty, grimy and certainly not prom ready we headed, without hast, to the house. In fact, we ran as fast as our feet would carry us. As we neared the house, we slowed, and then saw sitting on the porch, all decked out in tuxes with flowers in hand, our dates! We rushed past them and headed for the shower. I clearly remember washing the dirt from my hands and feet and thinking of my transformation. In a few minutes I would go from dirty farm urchin to dazzling princess. By the time we were dressed all traces of weariness had left our bodies. Oh, to have the energy we had when we were sixteen!

(How things have changed. My daughter, Ashley, would have *never* worked on prom day. After all when would she get in her hair appointment and her nail appointment?)

The next day would finally be Sunday. Ahh, we finally get a day of relaxation. There *is* rest for the weary and the tobacco farmers' daughter.

6) The Fields in spring

By late spring the tobacco plants were well established in the plant beds. The tractors would have been serviced and ready for another season. The fields had been "turned over" or roughly plowed the fall before and had been left latent during the winter. Now it was time to disc or "level" them out and make them prepared for the planting of those *precious* tobacco plants.

When the Southern States truck brought our spring supply of fertilizer, I was always mesmerized. Mesmerized because it was not ten or fifteen bags, it was *hundreds*. A flatbed truck full of 6-12-18 fertilizers was in our driveway. We would heave each bag onto a trailer and journey to the field. Each fifty to one hundred pound bag was hoisted into a bin attached to the side of our red farmall tractor. Row after row the fields were fertilized. I found hoisting those heavy sacks a strenuous job, but I *really* wanted to impress my daddy so I never complained, well almost never. He had no sons and I was always trying to prove to him that I could do any work that a boy could do. I could *sense* he was pleased even though he never verbally said anything. He didn't need too.

Freshly plowed land has a wonderful rich, earthy smell that I still appreciate today. I like to reach down and pick up and handfuls of freshly plowed earth, bring it to my nose and just breathe it in.

The fields not used for tobacco were prepared for other crops such as corn, hay, soybeans and our vegetable garden.

Spring meant a rebirth, a chance to once again start over.

Linda Hamlett Childress

With the warmth of the sun, the young tobacco plants begin to flourish, corn starts to sprout from the ground and *everywhere* you look is green. Any direction I turned my eyes would be filled with the breathtaking beauty and the newness of spring and a sense of hope for whatever was to come.

While all this preparation was going on we kept close watch on the developing tobacco plants. When they were the proper size, about six inches tall, and daddy said the moon was right; it was time to head to the fields for planting. By now it is late spring.

Mama driving the tractor while Cathy and I rode the planter

7) Time for Planting

The technology for planting tobacco has dramatically changed over the years. It has become much less laborious. Even though I was too young to remember the first method of planting, I can still describe it because of one of mamas' proudest possessions. It is a wooden peg. I remember it being smooth and shiny from years of use. Using the peg a five-inch hole was pressed into the soil. Young tobacco plants were then placed in that hole. It was slow and tedious work, but the job got done. Mama still uses the peg once in a while for transplanting. That means walking up and down the tobacco rows looking for plants that didn't survive the initial planting and then putting a new one in its place.

The hand planter soon took the place of the peg. It had a round opening at the top through which the tobacco plants were dropped, a space for water and a wooden handle across the top. The bottom was pointed and looked like some sort of mouth. When the handle was squeezed at the top, the mouth at the bottom clanked open. Tobacco plants were dropped one at a time into the planter. One person carried the heavy planter and another carried the plants. The planter was forcefully pushed into the ground usually with water splashing out. With a squeeze of the handle the plant dropped into the hole with a splash of water right behind it. This was also a painstakingly *long* and *laborious* process.

My personal experiences with planting involve a method that is still used today. No longer did you have to walk row after row, hour after hour, you got to *ride*! The two-person planter was attached to the back of the tractor and a long hose connected the planter to a water tank, on the side of the tractor. Our first planter was a green two-seater. When sitting on the planter your back was to the tractor and its driver. In between the two seats was a carousel that had rubber "hands" that would open and then clinch each plant. Above each seat was a bin in which the young plants were placed. We loaded up our bins. Cathy's bin was always *much* neater than mine. Her neatness and organization always paid off for her. Her planting went smoothly while I *wildly* tried to untangle my plants before it was my turn again!

Once our bins were loaded the fun began. Well, it was fun until our backs or rear ends started hurting. Anyway, we would jump on the planter and the driver, usually our mama, would raise us off the ground. When we arrived at the first row, the planter was lowered to the ground and the first plants placed in the "hands". I can still smell the diesel fuel from the tractor. As the tractor moved in the sandy dirt the planter "hilled" the row, positioned and watered the plant and also moved dirt around the base (of the plant), all at the same time. "*Wow*" This made our work *much* easier and *much*, more time efficient.

Many memories were formed on the back of that tobacco planter. You certainly were given a chance to bond with that person working next to you or you could just get lost in your own thoughts.

Planting tobacco in the early morning was the most unpleasant time. The plants were all wet and cold and what was worse was I knew I should have been sleeping in on this Saturday morning like an ordinary kid! There was also *no way* to stay warm and dry, which only added to my misery! Usually by midday things would start to look up.

The load of tobacco plants would be dwindling and the sun would be warm on our backs.

We did not measure our day by a clock because that did not matter. No one wore a watch! As long as there were crates of plants to be planted and sunlight, you kept working. We did stop for a "dinner" break and a few water breaks. *Everything* we did was placed second to getting the work done. Only when the last crate was pulled from the back of the trailer did we sigh with relief and then cheer with happiness. *Suddenly* we regained all the lost energy.

I remember, while planting late one evening, my sister, Cathy, and I singing from the top of our lungs. I can't remember what we were singing, but we were laughing and singing, our hearts filled with pure innocent joy. Recently I was complaining about all the work we had to do when we were growing up when mama reminded me of that afternoon of singing. I did not know that she was quietly enjoying our little serenade with a smile on her face and a contented peace in her heart.

Cathy, my oldest sister, (actually only 18 mos older) and I would often make up games to play while planting tobacco. We had to find something that would break up the monotony. Sometimes we would take turns planting solo. That is, one of us would fill our hands with plants and single handedly place them in the carousel while the other person got to hop *off* the planter. This was a chance to stretch your legs or just to "*act up*". Once in awhile our plant would fall out of the "hand" and not get planted. That was a "no-no", but one of us would get to jump off the planter and race to stick another in the ground. The other person had to keep the rhythm going on the planter! The tractor never stopped until it got to the end of the row.

The arms attached to the carousel on the planter were color coded red and yellow. We each picked a color. Mine was red. This kept the rhythm going. I can still hear that carousel clanking as we moved slowly down the row. It was to this rhythm that we sang many of our songs. Clink-chunk, clink-chunk, clink-chunk.

I remember the summer of the locusts. Some say they hatch every seven years and when I was sixteen it was the seventh year! They were the most *hideous* insects I had ever seen. I had just seen a movie about them that scared the wits out of me! On one particular spring day we were planting tobacco on the lower forty and the locusts were in rare form. They were screaming so loud that I could scarcely hear anything else.

My eyes widened as we neared the end of one row, which was near a wooded area. Hanging off the limbs in that patch of woods were *thousands* of locusts! My heart began to beat wildly, surely we wouldn't get too close to them, and surely they won't "*jump*" on me or get tangled in my hair! I *know* daddy won't take too long turning the tractor around!! Whew, it looked like we were home free, but wait! *Oh, no*, to my horror he started backing the tractor right smack into the tree limbs with all those locusts! I began screaming and trying to protect myself. Daddy was not happy about all that screaming and gave me a little "*talking to*". I think I scared him with the screaming. As it turned out, not one of those locusts fell on me or jumped off the tree and attacked me! We headed back down another row.

Placing the fragile green tobacco plants in the ground was only the beginning of our spring and summer "*vacation*". When we were not working in the tobacco

Linda Hamlett Childress

fields we were in the garden or doing house chores. We also had cows to be fed. There were always chores!

8) School Days and Summer Vacations

We hardly *ever* missed school, especially in the spring. If we stayed home we always ended up working! I was one of a small number of kids who didn't care how agonizingly long that school bus ride home was either. The longer the bus rides, the less time before dark there was to work! Our ride was longer than all the other kids. We were the first ones on and the last ones off. The bus could only save me until Cathy got her drivers license!

One warm spring day, after Cathy had her driver's license we were paged to the school office. At first the page made me fear bad news from home or I was in some kind of trouble. It was very nearly as bad as that! The principal told us mama had called and needed us to come home right away. The "help" had failed to "show up" for work and she needed us to plant tobacco. "No, I have a test!" "That's okay," the principal said, "you can take it another time". You see the tobacco farmers' kids were *unfortunately* excused to leave school to work on the family farm. Oh, *goody*! So Cathy and I got in that ugly green car of hers and hurried home.

To steer clear of work during the school year we found other activities. One of these activities was the Randolph-Henry marching band and before that the junior high band. All four of us played a musical instrument. Cathy, Janet and Kelly played the flute and I played the clarinet. I'll admit after eight years of playing I never did master that thing! What we *did* master to some extent was twirling baton. That I loved. My senior year I was head majorette and made sure we had plenty of practices and camp to keep *me* away from home as much as possible. Cathy and I were majorettes together and later Janet and Kelly were baton twirlers.

I must admit I was always a little envious, or truth be told a lot envious, of some of the other girls at school. On unusually warm spring days some of the girls were skipping school to stay home and work on their tans or they just hung out at the tastee freeze. They went to dance classes, gymnastics and piano lessons. In the summers they went to the local pool everyday or were off on a fun-filled vacation somewhere. The girls who did work had what I felt was a neat job like baby-sitting or working in an air-conditioned store. As an adult I no longer have any regrets about the life I had, but as a young teenager these things hurt deeply and I felt I was really missing out on life!

Vacation for us was an occasional weekend camping trip, which left me with memories of cold mornings, damp musty showers with moldy concrete walls, and my sleeping bag on top of rocks! I didn't want to leave the tent until at least lunchtime! We did at long last have a real family vacation. It was the only one we ever took together, I was sixteen years old. We took that vacation in the month of November 1979, not in July of course because that would have *interfered* with the tobacco harvest! My mama and daddy took the four of us to *Disney World*! I will never forget the sheer thrill and excitement I felt when I saw my first palm tree swaying in the warm Florida breeze or how much fun it was to stay in a hotel room where I could take a shower for as long as I wanted! After I was married my husband Steve got a lot of enjoyment and even chuckles taking me to new places. *Everything* was new to me, as I had had few life experiences. My first trip to Gatlinburg thrilled me to pieces!

I can't say I was the only girl in school who had to work on the farm. There were others, but most had brothers who did the heavy work and the daughters did the light work or stayed at the farmhouse. At my house there were no sons so the girls did it *all*! There were two girls in our school who actually had it worse than us. They didn't have any brothers either and the worse part was they lived on a dairy farm! Their work was all year long! They had to get up and go to the barn *every single* morning before school! At least *my* work was typically spring to late fall! My hat is off to any daughter of a dairy farmer!

In spite of all my whining, moaning and groaning my work experience has made me a better person. It helped me learn to work with people and helped me create a strong work ethic. As a dental hygienist, I spend much of my day telling people about my life as a tobacco farmer's daughter. I can't imagine what my life would have been like without my tobacco farming experience or just the farm life in general.

9) The Hilling Hoe

By the time school was out for summer the young tobacco plants were well established. As *they* grew so did the weeds around them. Weeds were an unwelcome thing in the tobacco field and trust me I *hated* to see them. I always hoped mama wouldn't notice them too soon but, lo and behold, there she was strolling from the barn with a very *nice* assortment of "*hoes*" in her hands! The hilling hoe is referred to as a "garden hoe" for all you city folk. Some of our hoes had handles as smooth as glass from years of wear and some might be turned into lethal weapons as the end might just *fly off* at any time.

Hilling hoes, oh how I detested hilling hoes. The only thing I did like about them was their ability to hold me up. You see, mama and daddy often caught me *leaning* on mine lost in yet another daydream, I'm sure.

Each tobacco plant had to be free from weeds, so plant after plant weeds had to be chopped or pulled. Briers were not fun to pull, so chopping them with the hoe was perfect. The blade of the hoe was quite sharp and all too often I chopped the weed *and* the plant! Whoops!! Quickly I glanced around to see if anyone was watching and then I would stick that rootless plant back into the ground and firmly pat some dirt around it. That plant would of course later die, but I didn't expect anybody to pull it up and look at the roots. It was simply replaced a few days later with a new plant. *No harm, no foul.* Ha ha, sneaky me.

After clearing the weeds from around the plant, dirt was pulled back around the stem to give it support. Many of the weeds were removed by plowing, which was done two or three times or until the plants got too tall. The problem with plowing was that the plow always covered the bottom leaves of the tobacco plant. *Personally* I felt to uncover the bottom leaves was a waste of my *precious* time, plus after a while my back started hurting! When my back started hurting, I found a *new* way to uncover those bothersome bottom leaves. However, this new way often got me into a heap of trouble. I discovered that I could somewhat effectively uncover the plants with my *feet*! Hey, no bending over and no back pain! Well, it didn't take old Harry Lee, my daddy, long to catch me and after a few futile warning calls he jumped from the tractor! (Uh oh, nowhere to run and nowhere to hide) *I was in trouble*, again. Cathy, my sister, recalls his exact words to me, "I'd better see you start bending your—back, girl!" Once again I was bending over, grumbling and uncovering those bottom leaves. Being rebellious or *hardheaded,* as my mama and daddy called it, I still used my foot when no one was looking.

Except for the blisters on my hands I suppose the hilling hoe was not *all* bad. Like I said, you could lean on it when you got tired or if you just wanted to daydream a little. Often after a long grueling day it felt good to stretch it across my tired shoulders as we headed home. I can still recall mama stopping on the road home to chop a stray weed with her hoe. I guess she couldn't help herself. It just gets in your blood!

Not long ago I got a chance to show off my hilling hoe talent. While working in my father-in-law, JS's garden, Bud, a neighbor, half jokingly commented on my obvious *ability* with the "garden hoe". I proudly let him know I

Linda Hamlett Childress

knew exactly what I was doing; after all I was a tobacco farmer's daughter!

"Chopping weeds"

10) Sucker Plucker

By the time the tobacco plants were hilled and hoed, plowed and chopped a few times it was usually late June or July. And it was time for the "sucker plucker". Meanwhile my friends were hanging out at the pool or off on a fun filled beach vacation, but not me! Okay, I know some of you have *no idea* what I'm talking about, so I'll just have to explain it to you.

After the tobacco plants become fully-grown they grow a blossom at the top of the plant and smaller sprouts at the base of each leaf called a "sucker". Well, these things are detrimental to the final weight of the plant. So all season mama collected jugs, jugs of all shapes and sizes. Clorox jugs, milk jugs or juice jugs. Any jug as long as it had a twist on top. When it was time to "top" (remove the flowers from the top of the plant) the plant, mama would punch tiny holes in all the jugs tops, so that it sprinkled the sucker plucker solution, not poured. She, bless her heart, did *all* the footwork. We just complained and waited for her to "make up" our jugs too. Mama mixed up the sucker plucker and filled *all* the jugs. Begrudgingly we'd drag ourselves to the field. We would start at the end of one field and row-by-row remove the flowers off the top of the plant. We would then pour "sucker plucker" on the stump where the flower once was. This chemical kept the flower from growing back. It was a little tricky pouring just the right amount of "sucker plucker". Too little and it wouldn't flow down the whole plant, too much and you had to fill your jug again too soon. Imagine heaving this jug up above you head hundreds of times in a day! Little wonder we were "buff" teenagers, now we call it working out! Some years later the "sucker plucker" was put in a large barrel attached the tractor. The tractor had a boom that extended over four rows. Four hoses that looked much like garden hoses fell from the boom. At the end of each hose there was sprayer nozzle just like the one you use to wash your car. This was an *enormous* improvement over heaving the heavy jug over my head. Now we simply walked with the pace of the tractor and squirted the sprayer! Sometimes the tractor driver started driving to fast and I would suddenly feel like Lucy in the "I Love Lucy" episode where the candy conveyor started moving a little to fast and she couldn't keep up. I'm sure I must have had the same dumbfounded look on my face!

OSHA would have been very unhappy with us, and the way we handled our chemicals. We hardly ever looked at the chemical warning labels. I wondered why my skin felt hot, my eyes watered and it really didn't taste so good! Well, fortunately years later my daughter wasn't born with two heads or anything!

11) Mishaps

My sister's and I proved wrong the old thought that boys were much rougher than girls, harder to raise and much more likely to get into mischief. We had *many* mishaps during our time on the farm, so many in fact that I will share only one from each sister. I will start with my own mishap.

Sunday's were often family visit days and this day was no different. My aunts, uncles and cousins came to visit. This particular Sunday my cousin, Carol Ann and I decided to play with the bicycle. Harmless, you might think. Well, not if it involved me! Carol Ann started off down the dirt road with me in hot pursuit, on foot. I thought it might be fun to hop off and on the back of the bike while she was "driving". Well, I jumped one too many times. The last time I jumped on I didn't "jump" off. My left foot became entangled in the spokes of the bike. "Stop", "stop", I screamed. Carol Ann thought I was laughing and she kept right on peddling! In fact, it seemed as if she peddled faster! Soon we were both falling to the ground; I just lay in the dirt and bawled, my foot a bloody mess.

My uncle Larry came to the rescue and carried me back to the house. Mama "doctored" me while daddy tried to make me feel better by saying, "stop that fuss, you all right, you all right". Mama kept looking at my foot and finally decided that I needed to see the doctor. In those days you didn't just *go* to the emergency room. The town doctor was called and we headed to his house. Wow, I was going to Doc's *house*!

Doc showed us in, took one look at my foot and had a "hissy fit"! "Why didn't ya'll tell me her toe was just barely hanging on?" Well, that was more information than I needed! I hadn't even looked at it yet. Now I was *really* scared and began to cry again.

We all went over to doc's office where he kept all his "scary tools". By this time I was cried out, my body numb. Doc sewed my toe back on and the big hole on the side of my foot. He then put a nifty bandage on and we headed home.

I milked my injury for *everything* it was worth, getting lots of extra attention from everyone. Daddy caught on real fast and read me the riot act about all the noise I was making as I hopped around the house. Okay, the drama was over, and I was soon jumping on and off the back of the bike, again!

Next, I'll tell about Janet's big mishap. Her mishap was an accident. She was just three or so and was sitting in the driveway playing in the dirt. She was playing in front of daddy's truck! He got into the truck, started the engine and proceeded to run over her! He happened to look in the rear view mirror and saw her. Janet was just lying there in the dirt crying. As I mentioned before the emergency room was rarely used, so they were off to see doc!

Tire prints ran along the right side of her body.

The doctor checked her over and declared her "fit as a fiddle". Her soft bones had saved her, and just maybe that angel on her shoulder had helped a little too. As it turned out Janet was fine, no broken bones, just some scratches and bruises.

I don't recall many mishaps with Janet. I didn't mess with her as much as I did Cathy, as Janet had that "Hamlett" mean streak and wouldn't think twice about throwing some silverware at you if she was mad! Nothing like a fork flying towards your head at warp speed!

Cathy's mishap involves me! Mama was down at the barn working and we were lucky enough to be at the house alone, being *good* girls as instructed. We hardly *ever* fought. Okay, that was a big fat lie! We were fighting over who knows what and I felt she needed a punch, so I gave her one! I don't fight fair, so I took off running with Cathy in hot pursuit! I ran for the first exist, which was the back door. I banged the door open with both hands and jumped all four steps to the ground. The door slammed shut behind me and latched!

Keep in mind that in those days doors were still made of glass. Cathy rounded the corner at warp speed intending too bang the back door open just as I did. That did not happen! She hit the door with both hands and *sailed through* the glass, down the steps and to the ground! "Oh, my goodness, she's dead", I thought as I turned to run. I had to go get mama, I had killed Cathy! I ran like the wind down to the barn to get mama. "Cathy's hurt herself bad", I cried. "What happened", Mama asked. I didn't give her a straight answer; as I knew I was about too get one of those whoopings I didn't deserve!

As it turned out Cathy had only some superficial cuts that required no medical attention. The broken glass in the door got the *most* attention that day. I managed to get out of that whooping, as mama couldn't decide whose fault it was!

The final mishap will be Kelly's. I didn't witness this one, but I have heard the story over and over again.

Kelly and Cathy were in the living room, watching T.V. and eating potato chips. Now you must understand that

Cathy is a neat freak and can't tolerate a mess. Well, Kelly dropped a chip on the floor and Cathy demanded she pick it up. "No", Kelly said. "Pick it up", Cathy yelled. Once again Kelly said "no", but this time she also took her foot and ground the chip into the carpet! Well, this set Cathy off!

Cathy jumped up and popped Kelly right in the face. The foot race began. Round and round the house they went and finally Cathy trapped Kelly on the back porch and *locked* the door! Kelly started banging on the glass door and screaming, "Let me in, Let me in". She banged one too many times. The last time her hand went *through* the glass. That wasn't the biggest problem. The biggest problem started when she jerked her hand *back through* the broken glass severing an artery!

Cathy rushed Kelly outside to the well and turned the spigot on. She tried to wash away the blood, but it kept gushing out. Frantically she ran with Kelly to a neighbor's house. Our neighbor was also our bus driver and she would know what to do. As it turned out the neighbor did the same thing Cathy did, she kept running water over it. The blood continued to gush from Kelly's wrist, as her face became ghostly pale.

Cathy knew this was "all wrong" and again took control of the situation. (Thank goodness). They headed back to the house, got into the car, and headed too the store, two miles up the road. As it happened, one of our local rescue squad members were there and quickly realized the severity of the situation. They all rushed to Brookneal to the local doctor. The doctor wasted no time as he called the rescue squad. He attended to her all the way to the emergency room where she was rushed into surgery to repair the severed artery. She had been minutes from death! Thanks to the quick thinking of John, the rescue squad member and the doctor, her life was saved.

Cathy cleaned up the potato chips!

My sisters and I had many mishaps, and somehow survived them all!

12) Whoopings

Until I watched a particular stand-up comedian joking about his mama and daddy giving him whoopings, I thought I had been an abused child. At *that* moment I realized that back in the 60's and 70's a whooping was the most popular form of discipline. We didn't have a game boy, a telephone or any other "things" to take away as punishment.

Whoopings came in many varieties depending on which parent was giving it. Mama was the fly swatter, switch and free-hand person. Mama would send us out for our *own* switch and then threaten us if it wasn't *big* enough. Well, what I found out was the skinny switches hurt *more* anyway, so I got wise and got the fat ones the first time! Boy did a swat from that switch sting. The fly swatter didn't hurt as much and mama usually just grabbed that as she chased one of us around the house. She could use that to add two feet to her reach! Lastly mama had a *mean* backhand. No not a tennis backhand, a *backseat backhand*. As she was driving down the road inevitably we would begin to fight in the back seat. Well, put four little girl's all-together in one small space and what do you expect? Mama would continue to drive down the road but would begin to furiously swat at us in the back. We usually started laughing as we watched mama continually *swat and miss* us. We were dodging her hand like mad!

Daddy used the old hand swat early on, but moved quickly to the dreaded belt. Once, Cathy and I were at the kitchen sink washing dishes. We didn't have an automatic dishwasher. Cathy *always* got uptight about getting soapsuds in the rinse water! So we started bickering and

A Tobacco Farmer's Daughter

soon heard daddy's first warning call, "ya'll better shut up in there". Daddy didn't like to be disturbed while he watched the weather report. Well, we kept bickering and then soon heard the second warning, "don't make me take my belt off"! Well, like always I could not shut my mouth and we heard *no more* warnings. "Dang, daddy was getting up from the couch and taking off his belt at the same time." (Too late; no place to run and no place to hide.) I always *wanted* to run, but daddy thwarted that thought by letting me know that my whooping would be much, much worse when I eventually came back! So, Cathy and I stood ramrod still as daddy stormed into the kitchen. There was one problem with this particular whooping. Every time Cathy got her swat on the butt the tip of the belt hit me! I was too *nervous* to move so I ended up being whooped *twice*! We later laughed till we cried about that particular evening.

As you can imagine four sisters *often* fought and argued. Once in awhile it would come to blows, but not often. We didn't really want to hit each other, just torment. Well, once in awhile if we were being especially obnoxious daddy made us go in the yard and duke it out. We *really* had to punch each other. Boy that took the wind out of our sails fast. Belts and switches didn't make us cry all the time, but actually hitting each other did. We only lamely hit one another and cried like the little girls we were. This "forced fight" didn't last long and it was awhile before we fought again. At least two hours.

One night my sister Janet and I were arguing in our bedroom. We were already in bed, but daddy could hear us through the bedroom wall. For whatever reason he thought *I* was the ringleader. I have no idea why he would think that! As usual daddy came storming in while *whipping off* that belt. I dived under the covers, head and all as he came in *swinging* that belt. It didn't take long for me to realize that it *didn't* hurt! Wow, all these covers were padding me! His belt made only a soft thud as he hit the covers. I started laughing so hard the covers shook and I'm sure daddy thought I was crying. Because he thought I was crying he only swatted a few more times. I think I must have laughed *all night*.

I did get out of one whooping. I had been playing in daddy's green Ford truck that was parked in the yard. I figured out if I took it out of gear and pushed the clutch down the radio would play without the key. So, I would go play the radio in the truck whenever I could. One day after I had been playing we looked outside when someone asked where daddy's truck was. Uh, oh busted! We found the truck lodged between two trees at the other end of the yard! I ran for my room and slide under the bed. There I stayed for hours until I heard mama calling for me. I didn't come out until mama told me I was *not* in trouble. What's the catch I wondered? Well, I found out the truck had lodged *perfectly* between the two oak trees and only bent the mirror! Whew, I dodged that bullet. That's the only time I remember *getting out* of a whooping.

Times have certainly changed. My daughter, Ashley has no recollection of ever having a whooping. Truth is after about age three we saw little need for corporal punishment. We simply took *things* away as punishment. We took her bike, her phone, and her sleepover privileges and later even took her car. *That* worked like a charm and we only had to do it once.

When I was a kid, the "stuff" was just *not there* to be taken away. What choice did our parents have?

So you simply got whooped!

TheTobacco farmer's daughter's

**Daddy & us girls
(Kelly, Janet, Cathy and Me)**

Linda Hamlett Childress

**My birthday party
(Me, Cathy, Janet and Kelly)**

13) Winter Fun

Before I get into all the spring to summer work we had to do, I wanted to tell you a little about what we did for entertainment in the winters.

With four daughters underfoot mama pushed us out the back door all season long. "Ya'll put your coats on and *get* outside", she'd say. It didn't matter how cold it was we always played outside. We had a few special places. One was a fallen tree at the edge of the woods. It had fallen and become lodged between two smaller trees. We would climb it and even take sticks and clear areas around it that we called "rooms". We had no other toys, just our active imaginations. If it was very cold we played in the calf shed. It protected us from the cold air and kept us outside, out of mama's hair. We would drag our dolls out to the barn and soon be fighting about who was going to play the mommy and who was going to be the daddy. We *all* wanted to be the "mommy".

As we got older we waited not so patiently for the first signs of snow. Snow meant loads of fun for the *whole* family. Mama said she knew when it was going to snow by the way the smoke traveled low to the ground from the chimney. Daddy said *he* knew it was going to snow when the remaining leaves on the trees turned upside down in the breeze. We just like kids today, waited anxiously for snow and hoped for a lot of it. Every year we would wake up to at least *one* decent snowfall. I would jump up each winter morning and peak out of the window. What a glorious sight to see. The tree limbs glistening white and heavy with snow. No ground and no road visible and *yes*, no school!

Mama didn't have to make us get out of bed on a snow day. We were out of bed, bundled up and out the door! When we were younger we would sleigh ride down one of our driveways that had only a slight grade to it. Mama would sometimes help us pack the soft snow so we could slide faster! We would play for hours before realizing how cold we were and go inside. There we would take off our wet socks and gloves. We placed them on the wood stove to dry fast so we could go back out soon. What usually happened were the gloves and socks just got *hot*! Oh, well we put them back on anyway and "hit the door running".

When we were older sleigh riding got a *lot* more exciting. We would climb to the highest point in the pasture and slide all the way down the hill, which was quite a distance. You had to be careful and make that left turn otherwise you would slide right onto the pond! As teenagers we started going on "night" sleigh rides. Wow, what fun! We always had to wait on daddy because he had the truck and that was an absolute necessity to get to our destination. When daddy got home from work we would rush him along, grabbing long johns and hats and gloves. All six of us would pile into the truck and head to the Mason's field. By the time the night was under way this had become a community event. Prior to everyone getting there people had already packed the snow down with the tractor. We needed light so they piled old tires at the top and bottom of the hill, poured kerosene on it and lit them. The tires would burn brightly all night long. We could see *and* we could stay warm. The only draw back from burning tires was the black, smut that settled all over everybody but that was a fine tradeoff for all the fun we had! We didn't have a traditional sled so we improvised. We slid on trashcan leads, garbage bags and the *highlight* of the night was five or six people sliding down the hill on an old car hood. You couldn't steer, but crashing was usually part of the fun. We quit being dare devils when Katie, our neighbor, broke her arm and we heard tale of someone breaking their *neck* riding the car hood down a hill. I miss those days of all night sleigh riding!

The winter was also a time when we all played board games at the kitchen table. Being cold natured I *always* chose the chair next to the woodstove. We played monopoly more than any other board games. We *rarely* finished a game of monopoly, especially if I was loosing! Okay so I wasn't the most gracious looser.

In the winter when it snowed mama always made us a special treat. Before the fresh powdered snow got trampled and dirty she would go scoop a bowlful. Mama would come back in and we knew what she was making, snow ice cream! She would add vanilla and sugar, mix it up and presto, we had instant ice cream!

At night in the winter when we weren't playing games or doing something in the kitchen we would be forced to quietly watch TV with daddy. We had no choice in shows so we ended up watching "Hee Haw" or "Lawrence Welk". Once in awhile if we got lucky we would get to watch an Elvis concert! We would all stare at that little black and white TV. We never had more than one TV in our house.

On Saturday night after the good "shows" were off the TV mama would play records on her stereo. Roy Acuff's, The Great Speckled Bird, album was the favorite. Daddy would lie on the couch, close his eyes and sometimes hum along. She would play records for hours and Daddy would occasionally give us a dance lesson. Teaching us to dance was very important to him. I can still hear him fuss at me for trying to lead! I still like to lead and I still like to dance.

Speaking of dancing, my mama and daddy could dance! Mama is 5'2" and daddy is 6'2" so they made quite the eye-catching couple. Many Saturday nights there would be a square dance down at the Aspen community center. Most people left their kids at home, but daddy refused. He said if he couldn't take the kids he didn't want to go and most of the time I *liked* going. I loved watching mama and daddy glide around the saw dusted wood floor. They were the best looking couple on the floor. I was so proud of them and they looked so happy. Sometimes mama would flat foot or dance around the outside of the floor with us girls.

I was always on the *lookout* during these dances. I was on the lookout for those "dirty old men" who needed a dance partner. Yea, I could square dance but I didn't *want* to dance with them! If I saw an old geezer headed in my direction I would slip downstairs to the bathroom or hide behind daddy. The only time I got caught was when I was square dancing with my own daddy and we changed partners. Drat, the old geezer had me and was squeezing all the air out of my body! We were pooped by the end of the night, but it was such fun. Thank goodness mama and daddy didn't leave us at home on Saturday nights.

Mama and Daddy 1965
In front of their three-room house

14) Craptown Store

"Camp town" store is *actual* name of the store, but I always felt "craptown" suited it just fine. There was certainly plenty of crap going on around there. It is situated off route 40, six miles outside of the big town of Brookneal. Actually there was no mall or even a grocery store very close by, so "Craptown" was a *Godsend*. If mama needed daddy for something that was the first place she called and he was typically there! In fact in the winter a good number of the men-folk were there. There was a great big wood stove near the front window and in the winter that was where everyone converged to *"talk"*. All we women know the men were *gossiping* but they just gave it a different name! I'll admit it was heart warming to walk into the store and see people gathered around the stove smiling and in high spirits.

On Friday and Saturday nights you could find some of the men playing cards and sneaking in and out of the door to their trucks for some *refreshments*. I remember mama calling up there to have daddy bring some milk home. She usually had to just go get it herself because it would be hours before daddy came home.

One winter we were all snowed in, fast becoming bored with all the usual snow day activities. Kelly and I got bundled up like Eskimos and with umbrella in hand faced the wind and the blowing snow for a trip to the store on foot. Slowly we walked the two miles to the store. It was tough going in the deep snow, but the reward at the end would be worth it, and it was. We arrived at the store, got us a drink out of the red coca cola box, a moon pie and sat by that smoking old wood stove to warm up. The only problem was we had to walk back!

This store was one of the places I learned about morals. This particular moral was stealing. I must have been six or seven years old and we had gone to the store for a few things. When no one was looking I slipped some candy in my pocket. When we got into the car mama saw me with the candy asked me where I got it. Uh, Oh. I couldn't think up a decent and blameless story so I folded, and told the truth. Well, she made me march back into the store, taking the candy with me, and apologize for stealing it. I was *so* humiliated and embarrassed; I didn't know what to do. I will say I *never* took anything from the store again.

One good thing about "Craptown" store was that we girls didn't have to *always* have money with us. We just said, "Put it on daddy's bill". There are hardly *any* places these days that still keep a tab for people. When I was older I really enjoyed that service since I filled my car with gas and put *that* on his bill. I didn't get to do that very often!

At a young age we girls started learning ways to make the almighty dollar. Mama and daddy paid us by the hour to work in tobacco, but we needed more money, so we scoured the ditches for empty soft drink bottles. The store would buy them back for five cents a bottle and then later ten cents. We felt like we had hit the jackpot. We loaded hundreds of bottles in the red wagon during our childhood and mama helped us haul them to the store. Mr. Guthrie, the storeowner, would tally the number of bottles, frown at the really *dirty* bottles that we had dug out of the mud, and then give us cold hard cash! We felt *so* rich. Heck, we must have had *three dollars each*! Before we left the store we would take a few coins and get us a 10-cent coke out of the old icebox. The cap was popped off the bottle on the side of the drink box. We had just purchased a soft drink with our own money and didn't even have to ask mama or daddy!

In the summertime the rickety store windows were thrown open, the heavy front door was propped open and everyone hung out on the porch. A fly swatter was always helpful for those pesky flies that flew in and out of the open windows and doors. There was an old-fashioned cast iron scale on the porch and people would weigh themselves or their kids. I never heard a single person around the store complain about there weight or discuss a diet. In the country, diet was not much of an issue that I recall. If you had seen what we ate you would wonder *why* we didn't have weight problems. We ate Vienna sausages, pork and beans and freshly cut bologna sandwiches. We also ate plenty of potted meat and crackers. To this day I eat potted meat and I don't *want* to know what it's made of!

At present my parents own "Craptown" store, but the doors are closed, as no one has been able to manage it successfully or with the charm it once had. I guess Food Lion and Wal-mart have taken away much of the need for the little country grocery. Those other places will never *ever* hold the charm or the memories that this old country store once held. I still hope that someone will come along and bring the old "Craptown" store back to life. I'll be waiting, ready to sit on that front porch with the sun warm in my face and a cold coke in my hand, diet coke of course.

15) Farm Animals

One summer I complained to daddy that we didn't have a *"real"* farm because we didn't have any chickens. We had a chicken coop with *nothing* in it. It was not long after I made that speech that daddy began work on that old coop in the backyard. It already had the nests and roosts so all daddy had to do was add chicken wire for the enclosed yard. We were then ready for our chickens and a few days later we had them! I was so excited because now we had a *real farm*.

It didn't take long for the novelty to wear off. Mama was soon nagging us to go feed the chickens, go break the ice off their water or go gather eggs! I now longed to have baby chicks, and then we would have a *real farm*. One-day daddy brought home a mean old rooster. He said we had to have one of those if we wanted babies. "Whatever", I thought as long as I had baby chicks.

Our rooster was a beautiful and proud animal. I was *very* frightened of him! He was very protective of his hens and decided he would *really* prove it early one morning. After we lost interest in the chickens' mama started taking care of them. Early one morning mama looked out of the window and saw that the chickens were out of the coop. She hastily put on her robe and headed outside to gather them up. This is when I heard her and so did daddy. A blood-curdling scream sent daddy *scrambling* out of the bed. He ran outside and immediately saw what the problem was. Mama was running for her life with Mr. Rooster right on her heels and he meant business. He was chasing her with *every* intention of sinking those sharp talons into her face. Finding a sturdy stick daddy swung and hit this crazy, out of control rooster. Yes, for all you animal advocates, the mad rooster died instantly. I guess it had to be the rooster or mama and mama won! Well, there went *all* my dreams of baby chicks and soon after each and every one of the chickens were gone. Well, I did at least have my little chicken farming experience!

The *best* chicken story happened only a few years ago. A banty chicken had found its way to our farm and decided not to leave. For a while it stayed safely in the tree, but slowly day-by-day daddy won this little chicken over. Pretty soon it was trailing daddy everywhere. Not long after this my uncle gave my daddy another chicken, a very *pleasant* banty rooster. This rooster was much less violent than the last! One gorgeous spring morning while visiting my parents a *loud* rooster's crow woke me from a deep sleep. The sound I was hearing seemed to be very close by. Sleepily I got out of bed to check out the crowing. What I found *truly* astonished and amused me. My daddy was sitting on the steps of the shed behind the house having quite a conversation with this rooster! The most amusing part was *every* time my daddy talked to the rooster *it* talked back! What a precious thing to observe. Daddy *really* loved that chicken. For some time after that there was confusion among the animals. They *all* acted in response to "here chick chick chick". If you say, "here chick chick chick", you can expect to see the dogs, cats, chicken and that rooster to come running! What pleasure it is to go back home. I *never* know what to expect!

The chickens were not our only farm animal experiment. We wanted calves, like *real* farmers. Daddy always bought our cows fully grown. We wanted our own baby calves that we could nurse and take care of. So one-year daddy came home with baby calves for each of us. Oh, boy! We had our *own* babies. They were each taken away from their mamas early and they each had to be fed with a bucket that had a nipple on it. Oh, how adorable they were. I gave mine a name and everything. For a few days I *jumped* out of bed and *ran* at take care of my baby. Well, just like the chickens, the novelty was soon worn off. I soon didn't *want* to get out of bed early and go feed it. I only wanted to feed it when I *wanted* to! More often than not mama fed the calf.

The problem for me was I found feeding the calf, *no fun at all*. It was a job-the bucket had to be clean and then powdered formula measured and mixed with water. This stuff was *so* sticky. I got very lazy and didn't mix mine very well and ended up with *lots* of sticky junk in the bottom of my bucket, which meant the poor calf got more *water* than formula. When the formula was mixed and in the bucket, I would peek from the side of the barn to see where the calf was. If I didn't see him I would as quietly as possible sneak to the barn to hang the bucket. It seemed that most of the time my calf would see me and would then charge towards the barn. Hard as I tried, I could *not* get that bucket hung on the door jam before that calf *head-butted* the bucket splashing formula everywhere. I was not too happy with sticky milk goop *all* over me. I must admit it was warming to see that baby calf eagerly nursing. Next was the task of getting the bucket away! Before the task was done that little black calf had sticky milk running down her face and all over me!

I couldn't end this chapter without talking about Cathy's pig. She loved this dirty old pig and took really good care of him. One weekend we had a cousin visiting from Kansas. It was a hot summer day and little Mike and I wanted to go visit Cathy's pig. We decided we would feed it too. Keep in mind we *meant* well. The pig ate *all* the corn we brought and so we thought it must be *very, very* hungry so we feed him more corn and then some more. What we failed to do was give him water. Hey, what did we know? We were just kids. Well, the next morning her pig didn't look so hot. He was bloated and he was *dead*. Oh, no! He ate himself to death. Cathy is *still* mad about her pig!

Mama had a pet pig too. Now *that* was one scary animal. It was big, red and *mean*. If I wanted to go outside I would first peak out the front door and make sure that pig was nowhere in sight. One time it caught me in the yard and sent me screaming as I ran through the yard. Now, mama *loved* that big pig and it loved her. Once it even tried to get.

In the house! Now that was taking it just a little too far for me.

We also had our dogs and cats over the years! Fuzzy, Brownie, Blackie, Shasta, Fee-bo, Rover and Prescious, the blind kitten to name a few. We miss all of them.

16) Moving *Pipes*

The day is scorching hot and the air is bone dry. Not a cloud in the sky. Sounds like the perfect summer day doesn't it? Not for us farm girls. We needed rain! Yes, these teenage girls are praying for rain on a summer vacation day! To the average teenage girl rain meant a ruined day at the pool, a disappointment. My sisters and I knew better.

When the ground becomes dry and dusty, Mama begins praying for rain and we secretly join in. Mama and daddy would appeal for silence as they stared at the TV and listened to the local weather forecast. We didn't *dare* utter a sound. If rain is not to happen that only leaves one thing, *set irrigation pipes*!

We always dreaded those now famous words from mama and daddy, "We're gonna lay pipes today!" You might be wondering what "pipes" are. They are called irrigation pipes and are made of aluminum and steel tubes with parts called "elbows, T's and sprinklers". We had piles of pipes and when it was time to position them in the fields we had to have a line of attack or some sort of plan. The pipes could only stretch so far so mama and daddy had to become engineers of sort, figuring out ways to make irrigating efficient and speedy.

The work of moving and setting up pipes was both laborious and yet satisfying. We hauled them to the edge of the tobacco field and laid them out in a pattern. Another filtered pipe was attached to the pump and positioned in the pond. When everything was all set I enjoyed watching daddy get ready to trigger that old pump. He would hand prime the pump and then he would whisper a prayer, (I'm sure), then turn that key. If all went well we would soon hear the drone of the motor as it came to life. Daddy then released the water to begin its journey to the field. We could watch the path of the water as it spewed from the pipes joints. Pretty soon the first sprinkler would emit a little water and a few seconds later it would be at full power. One by one and then row-by-row the field of sprinklers began to twist and turn spraying that precious water. It was a picturesque scene to behold. Art, country style?

Time and again there were minor flaws in our field of art. One sprinkler or the other would spray only a minute amount of water or none at all. This is when we would catch sight of daddy darting across the field evading the spray from the *working* sprinklers. When he reached the non-working sprinkler he reached into his pocket and retrieved a hairpin or what we called a "bobby-pin". With this bobby pin he would attempt to unplug the clogged holes. We thought it was *very* funny when the sprinkler *suddenly* started working and sprayed daddy in the face! I promise we didn't laugh! (wink)

I didn't laugh long for *I* soon got the pleasure of unstopping the sprinklers! Once wet with pond water I no longer cared. Running through the field from sprinkler to sprinkler became a game of sorts and also brought me some sense of accomplishment. To be able to fix something felt good.

Many times we spent the whole day irrigating tobacco fields. This I can't say I enjoyed. After the initial setup, the irrigation system was kept running for several hours or until mama and daddy felt the field had been satisfactorily wetted. The motor would then be shut down and a few pipes disengaged. After moving pipes for a few years we became creative and learned a way to move an entire row without having to disengage them *all*. This saved us a lot of time and work. My sisters and whoever else was working that day would line up and pick up an entire row of pipes at one time. Even though we were mired in mud to our knees we hoisted those, sometimes very hot, pipes over our heads and moved them to a dry section. We repeated this over and over until the field was finished or we ran out of daylight.

The very last pipe move was at dusk. My sisters and my work were done for the day, but that was not quite so for mama and daddy. After we had washed pond scum and mud away daddy was *still* running the pump. He would come up to the house for a little while, watch the news, and then he and mama would jump back into the truck. They had to go down to the pond and check on the motor. I can still hear the monotonous drone of the motor, the chic-chic-chic of the sprinklers and then the *sudden* silence. When daddy cut off the pump motor it cast an eerie silence over the farm. Once more we could hear the crickets chirping, the cry of the whippoorwill and occasionally the lonesome bullfrog, somewhere in the darkness. The day was finished.

Linda Hamlett Childress

Our irrigation pump

17) Blessed Rain and Scary Storms

A forecast of rain during a dry spell always brought us gladness. Mama would keep lookout at the kitchen window for storm clouds and then listen for the distant rumble of thunder. "A cloud's coming up", she'd say. Following the nearby path of the river, the storm rains would *regularly* miss our farm. My mama and daddy would be miserably disappointed. After a storm, that left us with only a few sprinkles, they would get in the truck and ride up the road to see how much rain the Mason's or the White's got. I'd hear daddy talk about the two inches "Reginald" got and the hailstones that "Darwin" got on that bottomland that we, thankfully, *didn't* get!

When those storm clouds *did* roll our way and bring us a bountiful rain, my mama would stand at the door and say, "*Oh, blessed rain.*"

Storms meant more than just *some rain* to my sisters and me. We were taught it was a *reverent* time and no one was permitted to talk. Four little girls lined up on the couch, quiet with the exception of a jab or two at each other. I imagine my mama used storm time to get a little peace and quiet!

One particular storm that I remember brought deafening thunder and intense lightening. It was quite frightening to four little girls huddled on the sofa. In the 60's our house was not "grounded". During this storm lightening struck close by our house and sent a ball of electricity shooting through the electrical socket in the wall. I'll never forget watching that *fiery ball* roll across the living room floor. I was never sure where it went when it vanished. This stray electricity may have been another reason we all had to get on the couch during storms. We also were not allowed to stand at the window, run water or talk on the phone.

If a storm rolled in while we were in the field we always got to go home. Lightening and metal hilling hoes *do not* mix. Lightening and metal don't mix, period!

I remember one storm in particular, a lightening storm; mama had gone down to the barn and we were watching her from the door of the house. She was working outside the barn when *out of the blue* a bolt of lightening struck the ground *right at mama's feet.* She was hollering and dancing as that ball of electricity rolled all-around her feet! I by *no* means felt she was in danger and I *could not* stop laughing. I *know* it could have been disastrous, but thankfully it turned out to be *just comical*!

So once again the rain would fall and the grass would become green again, but most importantly the tobacco plants were saved once more. Even now I adhere to mamas "storm rules".

Now, at the end of a dry spell when the rain gently falls, I stand on my own porch and softly speak mama's words, "*blessed rain, oh, blessed rain.*

18) Mama

All of my farm memories have one thing in common, my mama. I know *I* complained and whined about working, but mama in no way ever did. If there was a job to be done she just did it, *never* complaining.

She did *everything* for us. In the fall a pair of shoes was picked out for each of us from the sears and roebuck catalog. She didn't know our sizes so she would trace the outline of each of our feet on a piece of notebook paper. Mama sent the outline and all to Sears and soon we had our new shoes.

Because she had four daughters it was *impossible* to keep everybody in the latest fashions, so mama sewed. I can still hear the hum of the sewing machine and feel her fingertips as she pinned the dress here and there to fit. My friends *never* knew I had on a homemade jacket or dress. I even wore one of mama's creations on my wedding day!

During work mama did some comical things. Before the utilization of certain pesticides we had to physically pluck tobacco worms off each plant. Yes, real worms. *Big, green* worms they were. I personally haphazardly picked the worms off, but mama got *every* one of them. She literally turned over every leaf to check for those worms and then what she did *next* grossed us out. She pinched the worms' head off to ensure it died, and then threw it on the ground. Yuk, gross! I *couldn't* bring myself to do this so I sympathetically buried my tobacco worms in the sand. Mama's way was much quicker; I'm sure, but oh Yuk!

Mama always had ways to "*persuade*" us girls to get up for a workday. Like nearly *all* kids, early mornings were always the toughest times to get us moving. *"Girl's, its time to get up"*, she said nicely. *"Rise and shine girl's"*, she said a little more strongly. *"GIRL'S!!"* and finally, *"ya'll can get up now and get the work done while its cool outside or you can wait till it's hot"*, *"it makes no difference to me!"* When she put it *that* way we tumbled out of bed and swiftly got dressed. No matter what, she was out there with us. Not only was she *out* there, she had to organize and plan the workday. She filled coolers with water *every* morning. She would freeze water in paper milk cartons for the coolers the night before so the water stayed cool all day. Mama found the time to keep house, raise four daughters and have a large garden! Mama even played on our softball team.

Late one particular morning after working in the field, we headed home for what we called "dinner". Most people call that meal "lunch". Anyway, mama stopped by the mailbox and took out all the mail. As we walked she looked through the bills, letters and such. She came across one envelope from her doctor, which did not look like the usual *"you're okay"* letter. We all stopped and stared dumbfounded as mama just *looked* at that envelope. I think she knew without reading it that it was *not* good news. She opened the letter only to find a note asking her to call for another appointment. With a sober face and her chin held high she walked the rest of the way to the house and made that fateful phone call. I don't recall working anymore that day. In fact, I don't recall how *any* work got done the rest of that summer, one of the *longest* summers of my life. This was the time in my life when I first learned what anxiety felt like.

On her doctor's appointment day, fearing bad news, mama gathered all four of her little girls together and took us with her. There was twelve-year-old Cathy, seven-year-old Janet, five-year-old Kelly and I was eleven. We did no work that day. Mama also did something out of the ordinary; she took us *shopping* at Rose's in South Boston. We were really flabbergasted because it wasn't Christmas or anyone's birthday. Mama just wanted us all together for a special day. How *courageous* she was and how *afraid* she must have been.

Later that day, at age 32, my mama found out she had cancer.

A week or so after the diagnosis daddy took mama to the hospital for surgery. We girls didn't think too much about it since we thought she would be back in a few days *good as new*. This time in life was especially difficult for my younger sisters, Janet and Kelly. They didn't understand what was really going on. They wondered why daddy was always gone or why he was just sitting in the rocking chair on the porch, staring off into the distance. This was, I believe, a reality check for daddy. It was a reality check for *all* of us. Mama was at all times taken for granted.

Mama had her surgery and the cancer was removed, but things would not remain so simple.

After mama departed for the hospital people began to stream in. In the country if you have a death, a wedding or someone gets sick people *really* turn out to help. The ladies from Mt Carmel Church came by often with food. Mama's brother, David, and his wife showed up, parked their RV in the side yard and tried to help. Daddy's sister Penny also stepped in to care for us four girls. *That* was a feat in itself!

While people poured in to help take care of us girls mama was finding out her cancer had spread. She would face yet *another* major surgery and would *not* be coming home in a few days as we once thought. Since she couldn't come home we were taken to the hospital to see *her* only to be turned away. Except for 12-year-old Cathy, we all were told we were *too young* to go inside the hospital and visit mama. Cathy was the *only* one who was allowed to see mama and touch and hug her. I *still* feel the hurt. I tried not to let my pain show, but inside I was dieing. I wanted to see her. Daddy would park the truck under mama's third floor hospital window so we could at least *see* her. We could see her standing there at the window waving softly, weeping. Kelly and Janet would begin to whimper and then sob. They just *didn't* understand why mama was up there and couldn't come home and *we* couldn't go to her. Hearing five-year-old Kelly cry hurt my heart the most.

Mama would soon have her second surgery with *good* news to follow. They had removed *all* her cancer and she would come home soon! Even though relatives, especially my daddy's sister, Penny, had taken care of us we wanted *our* mama back! Little did we know she would come home *different* than when she left.

My sisters and I expected mama to come home and pick right up where she left off. We needed her to cook and clean for us. Daddy needed her back on the farm keeping the books and working in the field. What we saw *stunned* us all.

Mama came in the door at first to hugs and kisses and then *shocked* stares from us girls. She could not stand entirely upright because of the incision that ran hipbone to hipbone. Hanging from her side was a "bag", a catheter bag that *always* seemed to burst open in the middle of the night causing her even *more* anguish and misery. How frustrated she must have been when she arrived home. Instead of lots of tender loving care, we expected her to go right back to her *"duties"*. If I had been older and less selfish I would have waited on her hand and foot. I would have *insisted* she stay in bed while *we* took care of things. I guess we were just too young to *really* understand. What I do understand is mama was our life. Mama is *still* our life.

Mama did heal and thrive. She has been cancer free for *thirty* years. Thank you Jesus! Thank you mama. I love you.

Linda Hamlett Childress

Mama and her mama 1956

19) The Garden

Besides having the tobacco fields to work, we also had a large garden, usually near the house.

Just when we thought we were home free mama would start hollerin about the garden. "Girls, I need some help in the garden", she'd yell. We, with reluctance, would join her there. Most days we just had to pick green beans, butter beans or tomatoes, but once a year it was the dreaded "potato pickup day". You might think that sounds trivial. We didn't have a few potato plants; we had hundreds, which required a tractor to dig up. Tub after tub we hauled those spuds out of the garden. When we thought we were finished, daddy would run the plow over *one more time* and uncover what seemed like thousands more potatoes. We thought it would never end!

The garden also reminds me of happy times, like sitting in the shade of the porch with my grandma shelling peas or going over to the neighbors house to help her shuck corn. We always got an ice cream or a piece of cake for helping.

Mama sometimes took us to cut "creasy salad", a leafy green that grows randomly in fields or on the edge of the road. Mama would watch for it along the roads all as she ran errands up and around the community. She would cut bags of it, take some home, and take the rest to a neighbor or someone from church. We always knew when she was cooking it because it *stunk to high heaven!*

What vegetables we didn't eat fresh, mama canned or froze; we always had plenty of food in the winter. Mama always had a pot of vegetable soup or a crock- pot of pinto beans simmering. The garden brings back warm memories of times past. These days it's cheaper to go to Wal-mart or Food Lion for vegetables, but there you won't capture the family togetherness that the old-fashioned garden brings.

20) Lessons from Daddy

There are *always* lessons to be learned in life. Many of my life changing lessons were learned on the farm and *many* times daddy was the teacher. Many of these lessons we have carried into our lives as working adults. We learned work ethics.

One particular lesson stands out in my memory. This is the year Cathy and I became *bona fide* business owners. We were aged seventeen and sixteen. Daddy called Cathy and I to talk to him one day and told us he would be giving us 1.5 acres of land to grow our *own* crop of tobacco. I don't think daddy thought the venture would amount to much, but Cathy and I were *very* excited and took this challenge very seriously.

We participated in *every* step. We didn't want to pay workers so we did as much as we could ourselves. We babied that field of tobacco plants, often working after the "normal" hours. We checked our field over every day to make sure everything was coming along without any problems.

Daddy deducted expenses such as fertilizer, seeds, workers pay and such so we would have a *real* knowledge of the business side of our venture. This was *truly* sobering.

All summer we carefully tended our small crop. It was *ours* and now work and money had new meaning.

At the end of the growing season we were exhilarated. It was now time to harvest our crop and take it to market. As we harvested daddy kept track of what tobacco came from our field. He was very fair to us.

On market day Cathy and I could hardly contain our excitement. We thought we would have to wait until daddy came home to find out how much money we had made. This was not the case. Daddy *insisted* we come along to the market. He wanted us to see this venture through to the end. *Wow*, we *girls* were going into the *manly* world of the tobacco market!

The distinct smell of cured tobacco filled our nostrils as the big warehouse doors opened to allow our ton truck to enter. Each pile of tobacco was hoisted off the truck and placed on a large scale to be weighed. After being "weighed in", the piles were tagged and placed in one of the many rows of tobacco inside the warehouse. Each farmer always knew where *his* tobacco was.

Farmers in their coveralls and John Deere caps stood around smoking and trading stories while keeping a close eye on the location of the graders and buyers. The graders were the people who determined what type of tobacco you had and how good it was. They then placed a grade on the pile. The buyers came along behind the graders, looked at the grade that had been written on the tag and then put a price on or bid on that pile of tobacco. When they got near our piles of tobacco daddy said, *"Ya'll go over there and sit on top of your piles and let the buyers know it's yours"*. I was nervous and didn't really want to do this, but I trusted daddy's judgment. Lo and behold sitting on those piles did pay off. As soon as the buyers got near us my sister blurted out, *"this is our tobacco, and we raised it ourselves"*. I remember the buyer "grinning like a mule eatin briers" and saying, *"Well, lets give these little ladies a real good price"*. They proceeded to increase the price per pound by ten cents! Wow, what a feeling! Being a *girl* tobacco farmer

A Tobacco Farmer's Daughter

paid off that day! Our long, hot summer workdays had paid off in a big way. We headed to the bank and deposited most of our money, keeping a little out to celebrate with.

That summer we learned the business aspect of farming as well as a little *politics*. Most importantly we learned the values of hard work, not just in the form of a paycheck but also in how we felt about ourselves as people.

Thanks to daddy we learned that there is much value in a *job well done*.

21) Daddy's Antics

My daddy had always been a bit of a comedian. He has an uncanny knack for making people laugh. I am happy, I think, to report that I have inherited that personality and that need to make people laugh. I have often said, *"as long as I live, my daddy will never die"*.

One of daddy's antic's I remember well.

Even though he repeated it often I *always* fell for it. Daddy would *suddenly* get up from the couch and rush to the window of the front door. For the *longest* time he would stand, strain his neck and stare out of that window like he was looking *at* something. Finally I couldn't stand it *any* longer and I would get up to see what was keeping his attention at the window for so long. Well, guess what? It was *nothing*. Daddy would howl with laughter and slap his leg. *"Ya'll always look; you can't stand not knowing, can ya?"* I'd then huff back to whatever I was doing.

One night when I was about fifteen we decided to give daddy a taste of his *own* medicine, sort of. He came home one night with a few "nips under his belt" and feeling fairly tipsy. My sisters and I were in the living room and I had, in my possession, a *big, black plastic spider*. I tied a long piece of thread to it and jumped on the chair with my feet tucked under me. On cue my sisters and I started screaming and yelling and of course daddy came quickly to see what the fuss was all about. We were jumping up and down pointing to that big black spider in the floor. Daddy focused as best as he could and tried to balance. He raised his foot high and slammed it hard, just as I made the spider move a few inches. He *missed* it! I yanked that string making the spider move. Tried as we could, we failed to keep a straight face. Before long *we* were the ones laughing hysterically and we let daddy know that *this time* the joke was *finally* on him.

As I tell that story today, it *still* makes me laugh.

Daddy was *always* up to something. When playing cards he was notorious for cheating all the while keeping a not so innocent look on his face.

What I remember most about daddy (he still does this today) is his comebacks for *everything* you said. Once I told him he was nosey and that *"curiosity killed the cat"*. His reply immediately was, *"and satisfaction brought him back!"* What could I say to that? Another time I told daddy that "*beauty was only skin deep*" for which he replied, *"but ugly is to the bone!"* There was and always *is* a comeback from my daddy.

All I can say is, hmmm, I'll be thinking of something.

22) Silence

The one thing I miss most about being on the farm is the sounds, the early morning chirping of the birds to the late night sounds of the bullfrogs, and crickets, to the complete *silence*.

From my bedroom I could hear the lonely sounds of a not so far off, freight train. On summer nights I could hear *everything* from my open bedroom window. The summer breeze caused the curtains to flutter and through that open window I could hear mama and daddy talking or just the scrape of the lawn chairs as they sat and enjoyed the tranquility of the night. I recall lying snugly in my bed in winter and hearing the crackle of the logs in the wood stove.

Some days I would take lingering walks around our farm. Every step I took seemed to echo in the silence. I knew even then that this was an extraordinary place to be.

While taking my walks I would search for special places to *pause*, places just to sit down and be all by myself. My breathing was sometimes the only thing that I could hear. Many times I even thought I could hear my own heart thumping in my chest. It was and is sometimes unnerving to sit in all that silence. It now makes me realize how much noise and chaos that is all around us in our everyday world. We are all too caught up in our fast paced lives. We need to stop and seek this silence, this peace and tranquility that, for me, only the farm in the country can provide.

There on the lower forty I discovered time to *"find"* myself and time to *really* talk to God. I reckon he must love this farm as much as I do!

23) Soul Searching

No country story would be complete without a chapter about church. *Everything* I did in my twenty years on the farm was somehow wrapped around Mt Carmel Methodist church. There we prayed for rain, we prayed for the sick and we prayed for our souls. We prayed for everything and everybody.

When we were little girls I remember mama getting us ready *every* Sunday morning. Finding socks and shoes for four little girls must have been nerve racking. We were *never* given a choice about going to church. We had regular service on Sunday, *every* Sunday and after church daddy would take all of us to "Willard Austin's", a restaurant (and beer joint) just outside Brookneal. Daddy would make us wait in the car while he went in to get us Sunday "dinner". Hotdogs with chili is what I had and it was *so* yummy. Sometimes we went to the tastee freeze in Phenix for ice-cream sundaes. Yes, Phenix. Phenix, Virginia.

On Easter Sunday mama would dress us up in our homemade dresses and new white patent leather shoes and go to the sunrise service. Later we got our surprise from the Easter bunny. Four little Easter baskets lined up on the couch. I loved Easter Sunday and knew what it meant early on. Singing the song, "Up form the grave he arose", always made me have renewed hope in life.

In the summer we had Bible school, which I *loved*. I continued to go until they finally kicked me out at age sixteen. I loved marching in to the bible school music, the crafts and of course the snack time of cookies and Kool-

Aid. When I was older I loved going because I got out of work in the tobacco field for a few hours!

In grade school I was, along with my sisters, a member of the junior choir. That was fun, but I *longed* to be in the coveted senior choir. They got to go skating and bowling and did all the fun "older kid stuff". They also got to do special services at church. My day *did* finally arrive and I became a senior choir member. Now I could go skating and bowling and have lead parts in the Christmas play!

As I got older I wanted to go to church less and less. Our choir director, Mary Ellen Hamlette, made it next to *impossible* to miss church. If you did happen to miss she was on the phone that same day finding out what was wrong and then making you *promise* you'd be at choir practice that same night. We very seldom missed church.

In junior high I started playing church league softball. One of the rules to play was you had to attend Sunday school on a routine basis or you didn't *get* to play. I loved softball and prided myself on my softball talent, so I went on to Church.

This was *another* tricky way to keep us youth coming to services.

One Saturday night Cathy and I sneaked in very, very late. We turned into the driveway, shut off the lights and killed the motor of the car. We slipped in the front door and quickly into bed. No one was up and no one knew how late we were, or so we thought. The next morning was Sunday and we had only had a few hours of sleep, but mama was yelling, *"get up, its time to get ready for church!"* Oh, no! We didn't *dare* tell her we had been very late coming in. So off we went to church with no rest. To make matters worse MaryEllen and mama made us sing in the choir!

I realized many years later that mama knew all along how late we were. This was her punishment for us and we didn't even know it!

Every year we had a week of revival. A time to rid yourself of all your worldly sins and start over! It never failed to amaze me how the guest preacher could lure me to the pulpit at the end of that week of services. By the end of the week I was fully convinced that I was the biggest sinner in Charlotte County and if I didn't follow that "pull in my heart", I might go to hell! So up to the pulpit I'd go. It was and always is hard to go up in front of all those people. You know they are starring at you and wondering what sin you committed! Once I got up there the preacher man always comforted me and made me know I had done the right thing. *Leaving* the front of that church was always liberating and my heart always felt good. I know now that it was indeed a true spiritual calling as the choir sang, "just as I am, without one plea", the invitational song.

As an adult I'm beginning to realize how much I learned in church during those early days. I learned many, many bible stories and didn't really realize *how* many until I was an adult. As I get older I depend more and more on my spiritual rearing in that tiny church in Charlotte County.

A Tobacco Farmer's Daughter

Mt Carmel Methodist Church

24) Pulling Tobacco

Around mid-July the tobacco plant was fully-grown and ready to *leave* the field. It couldn't leave the field by itself; people had to "pull" it. Each week the bottom-most leaves were pulled. You *knew* which leaves to pull off. The ones that were ready had a slight yellow tint to them.

On "pulling day" daddy usually left the house around six a.m. to go around and pick up the hired help. Many of these people did not have cars and needed a ride. By the time daddy got back with the "help" the others had arrived and we girls were *already* headed to the barn.

In the early days the tobacco was pulled in the field and placed in "slides" that were pulled to the barn by mules. The slides were brought from the field to the barn where the women folk usually were. For a while I thought we at the barn had the hardest jobs. I finally got my chance to be a "puller" one morning when we were short on help. I had watched the men pull tobacco for years and felt this would be a piece of cake. What I found was *instant* back pain from the constant bending over, pulling those bottom leaves! Besides the back pain I got cold and wet right away and soon had sticky tobacco wax on my hands AND under my armpits! After that day I avoided the "pulling" part of the harvest process.

We did have a couple of men to put the tobacco in the barn. At the barn the leaves were handed to a person who was tying it to a stick. The stick had been placed across a "horse" which was a wooden contraption that held the stick. If you could tie fast you were considered skilled and you were highly sought after as a worker. The completed stick was then passed off to a person waiting in the barn.

In later years we purchased a "looper" also called a "stringer". This was much more efficient than the old-fashioned hand tying. With this apparatus four people were utilized and two were inside the barn. Tobacco leaves were removed from the slide and slapped on a shelf above the looper. The "end person" placed a bed of leaves called the "bottom layer"; the middle person laid the tobacco stick. The stick layer was usually one of us girls. It gave us a job at a very young age. We were so short we had to stand on cinderblocks to be able to lay the sticks. If the other people on the line got behind the stick layer was expected to pick up the slack. The *third* person in the "looper line" laid the top layer of leaves. As you must have guessed this machine runs continuously like a conveyor. After the leaves had been layered they were run through a sewing machine type contraption. It had a very large needle that had a heavy string through it. It looked much like a large sewing machine. More than once someone got his or her hand pulled into the stringers needle. The needle would sew their hand right into the tobacco leaves! Yikes!

After the layers were sewn together the string was chopped and the stick, loaded with tobacco, was ready to be moved to the barn.

While we worked at the barn the field workers tried very hard to make sure we *didn't* catch up. They liked to fill *all* the buggies and have us back-logged. If all the buggies were at the barn then they got a break in the field!

Mama and daddy knew exactly how many "buggies" it would take to fill a barn. I always hoped we were doing only one barn each day.

Over the last twenty years tobacco processing had continued to become more time efficient *and* easier. The "looper, stringer" is now obsolete. The "in thing" now is called the "*bulk barn*". The tobacco is brought to this bulk barn and basically just *thrown* into a "box". This allowed much more tobacco to be brought in from the field in a single day. I liked this much, much better. It was so much faster and easier!

Often our "pullers" didn't put in an appearance and we girls had to do *everything*! We had to take the tractor to the field, pull the tobacco, load it into the buggy, take it back to the barn…okay you get the picture. These were *tough* days. I did feel some sense of accomplishment at the end of the day.

When the "help" continued to "*no show*" daddy got irritated and then desperate and that's when we were first introduced to the migrant worker. People yell and scream about *all* the jobs going to migrants, but the bottom line was we needed people who were *reliable*. When it was time to go to work we needed to know that we had some help, not be unsure of what each workday would bring! What we found with the Mexicans was dedication and hard work. They had families in Mexico who lived in houses with dirt floors and were waiting for money from the USA to feed their babies and many times their aging parents. At the break of day we *always* found the Mexicans waiting, ready to work. They *never* complained about the heat or how long they had to work on a given day. They *never* failed to "show".

While on the subject of migrant workers, I would like to clear something up. *Legal* migrants were and are *not* treated

A Tobacco Farmer's Daughter

unkindly or unfairly, not on our farm anyway. We had three trailers on the farm where they lived. Each trailer had to be government inspected every year. Each worker had to have his own bed and closet area. They had a kitchen and hot and cold running water. They were *"living large"*. After all, they had *none* of these luxuries in Mexico. Their salaries were also government controlled. Once each season daddy took the Mexicans to Kings Dominion and weekly he took them to town to shop for essentials and little trinkets to send home. He always treated them with kindness and respect. When they had bad news from home daddy grieved with them and with joyful news daddy celebrated with them. So don't believe all you read or see on TV. The exception to all this may be the *illegal* migrant. Illegal migrants *open* themselves up to unfair treatment and it is usually from unscrupulous farmers who care *little* about people in general.

Tobacco farming has changed significantly over the years, from mules and slides to tractors and buggies, from sticks to boxes, from local workers to migrants. Even the plant beds are becoming obsolete. They have now been replaced with climate-controlled greenhouses. Mother Nature has less control of a least one step!

Even with all the advances in tobacco farming the future of the tobacco farmer is unsure. As a dental hygienist I preach to people daily about the dangers of smoking. I in turn tell them that I grew up on a tobacco farm! It's a double-edged sword for me. It was a lifestyle for me and still is for many others and I know how much the industry helps our economy. The anti-tobacco people don't really look at the economic effect of losing the tobacco industry they just ride that particular "blame"-wagon, the bandwagon of the moment. Let's face it; the tobacco industry does not put that cigarette in people's mouths, it's a choice, just like over-eating or drinking alcohol.

My hope is that research will continue to find uses for the tobacco plant and our local economy won't continue to suffer. I'm afraid it won't happen *soon* enough. Virginia Tech continues to study uses for tobacco so there may actually be hope for the future.

1979 Daddy working at the new bulk barn

A Tobacco Farmer's Daughter

Daddy and the Mexicans

Linda Hamlett Childress

25) The Packing House

In the early to mid 1960's I was too young to do any bona fide tobacco work, but I still have vivid memories. One of these memories of mine centers round the "packing house". The packinghouse was a tiny, weathered gray wooden building with a tin roof. It had two rooms, a covered shed and a pit. A dark, musty, cold pit! I was *very* afraid of that shadowy hole. Under the heavy hatch door was a flimsy wooden ladder attached to the red, clay wall. The floor of the pit consisted of the same red dirt as the pit walls. When light was needed a single solitary bulb on a cord was dropped down. You might wonder what this horrible space was used for, besides breeding snakes and housing vampires! It was used to "*bring*" already cured tobacco in "*order*". Now you want to know what that means right?

Well, after tobacco is taken out of the field and put in a barn it is heat cured. It is taken from green to brown. After it was cured it often hung in the barn or was stacked in the packinghouse until it was time to be sold. While it was hanging or lying there it often got dry and with the slightest pressure crumble into dust! Not good if you want to sell it! So, the damp pit was where we put it for a few days. Moisture goes back into the tobacco leaves and they become "pack able" again. Then we *packed* it, get it? Luckily I was older before I was forced down that dank, gloomy hole in the ground. I was always scared stiff, afraid I would grab a snake or that somebody might think it humorous to close the pit door on me! That would have been a great joke, but not on me!

Upstairs in the packinghouse was a different story from the pit. I found it quite cozy, especially on those chilly winter days. Inside the main room were a solitary storm glass window and a small, tin wood stove. I remember the radio playing WODI, a local country music station and Madeline Lane, our neighbor who was working with us, laughing and telling stories. She always had a long cigarette dangling from her lower lip. As I listened to mama and Madeline laugh and talk I snuggled on a mound of old burlap sacks. The recently stoked wood stove made the room warm and toasty. Life was good. Not a worry in the world.

Inside the packinghouse, the softened tobacco leaves were tied and placed in burlap bags before being taken to the Gold Leaf Warehouse, a tobacco market in town. I still, after all these years, remember how to "tie" these bundles. I'll try to give you a brief description of how this was done. This will bring back memories for you tobacco farmers, and maybe confuse everyone else! Well, the tobacco was taken off the four-foot wooden stick that it was cured on. That could be an entertaining job all by itself. If you pulled the string slowly and just right all the leaves would just *fall* off the stick, no knots to break and no breaking of the stems. Once the leaves where off the stick you would grab a handful in one fist and hold them firmly at the top. You then look around you for the one perfect golden tobacco leaf. This leaf was then wrapped around the top of the bundle and tucked in between the leaves to secure it. It was time-consuming work, but mama always seemed to relax and be most contented during this time of the year.

While the "women folk" and children were in the packinghouse daddy would often come by in his Ford pickup and bring us snacks from Camptown store, frequently referred to as "craptown" store. Once, he came by the packinghouse and brought my sister Cathy and I tiny little plastic dolls. My doll had a plastic pleated skirt and a plastic shirt that snapped on. Her miniature arms and legs were held together by tiny rubber bands. I *loved* that tiny gift and I so long to have her now. What happiness it brought to me that day. Thanks daddy!

As small children, we didn't have to stay inside the packinghouse to find entertainment. Being outside in the wide-open space was always an adventure. There was a well-worn path between the outer wall of the packinghouse and the overgrown cocker berry bushes that lead to a pasture. The pasture leads to the woods and a small trickling stream that was the home of more than a few crawfish. We stayed on the go for *hours* and mama never had to be anxious about where we were or worry that someone had stolen us. The rumbling of our hungry stomachs always seemed to bring us back to home base or that need to hang out by the wood stove for a while to thaw out. Then all we needed was a nap! Too young to work in the packinghouse! Ahhh! Those were some of the good ole days; they just didn't seem to last quite long enough.

A Tobacco Farmer's Daughter

The Packing House

26) Summers End

With this chapter, I will, with a heavy heart, close. To me this is a fitting end to all my stories.

Every year, while I lived on the farm, the end of summer would leave me with a sad somewhat empty feeling. The stark tobacco stalks have been bush-hogged and plowed under, no longer visible. The fields now stand empty and void of summer color or feeling. The tractors sit quietly under the shed, waiting for winter. The barns stand empty, sad? Waiting?

The leaves on the trees have begun to loose their brilliant summer gloss and soon they will turn *Hokie* orange and maroon, then brown, and fall softly to the ground.

I am all too aware that another precious year of my life has slipped away, but sure as the sun rises in the east, there *will* be another season of tobacco farming. Or will there be? No one knows what the future holds for the tobacco farmer. All I can say is after leaving the farm twenty years ago I still can't let go of, or forget, the memories. The end product of tobacco may be a health hazard, but my tobacco farm upbringing was a *lifesaver*. As a teenager I didn't have time to do drugs or develop an alcohol problem. My mama and daddy knew where my sisters and I were most nights. We were safe.

I have spent the years since I left the farm trying to, "catch up with the Joneses". I wanted to *be* somebody. I went back to school to get a job that made more money. I finally got that big house in the fancy subdivision, a nice car, and the expensive jewelry. I have spent vacations in New Orleans and at the beach and many other places. I kept *waiting* to finally *arrive*. What I have now realized is that I will never change that person within. No amount of money or things can change that inner self, that personality that was molded on that tobacco farm. I will always be that country girl from Charlotte County.

I had already arrived; I just didn't know it.

As an adult I try to give my job 100%. My mama *always* told me that I could *do* or *be* anything if I just put my mind to it and *worked hard.* I know now that she was so right. She would expect nothing less.

My heart, soul and spirit will *always* wander those sandy fields and when *all* is said and done, and the farm is no more, I will still have, tucked safely in my heart, my memories and my *stories*.

Yes, you can take this girl off the farm, but you will NEVER take the farm out of this girl!

Linda Hamlett Childress

1965-Me and Cathy
Easter

Mama checking the barns

Linda Hamlett Childress

Taking a stroll at the end of the season
Mama, Jamie and Ashley

A Tobacco Farmer's Daughter

The Tobacco Farmer's daughter

Linda Hamlett Childress

H.L.
1962

About the Author

Linda was born one of four daughters and raised on a tobacco farm in rural Charlotte County, Virginia. After countless times of telling her humorous farm stories, she decided to combine her love for writing with her need to tell her stories and put them on paper for all to share.

This book is for all who have grown up in the rural tobacco farming community and share her memories of country living or for those who just want some idea of what tobacco farm living in the 60s and 70s was like.

Linda currently works as a dental hygienist in Roanoke, Virginia. She enjoys hiking, biking and kayaking. Linda resides with her husband Steve, and daughter Ashley on Claytor Lake.